NERVE / The New Nude

Edited by Genevieve Field, cofounder of nerve.com

CHRONICLE BOOKS
San Francisco

I am grateful to the photographers and models whose talent and trust are the body and soul of this book.

To Meredith Kovach and all of my colleagues at nerve.com, countless thanks for helping to shape *Nerve*'s vision of a "new nude." My appreciation also goes to Neeti Madan for placing this project in the gifted hands of Sarah Malarkey, Shawn Hazen, and Anne Bunn at Chronicle Books.

Finally, I would like to thank Theodore McCann, who sees differently and inspires me to do the same.

—Genevieve Field

Many thanks to the authors who lent their keen insights to the photography in *Nerve: The New Nude*. Some of their introductions have been modified or abridged for this book.

Introductions to Thomas Carabasi, John F. Cooper, Frédéric Goudal (FiLH), Thomas Karsten, Richard Lohr, and Holger Maass © Lorelei Sharkey; Introduction to Elinor Carucci © Minna Proctor; Introduction to Renee Cox © Dwayne R. Rodgers; Introduction to Katrina del Mar © Lisa Carver; Introductions to Andrew Einhorn and Peter J. Gorman © Emma J. Taylor; Introduction to Nan Goldin © Grady Turner; Introduction to David Levinthal © Amanda Griscom; Introductions to Leslie Lyons and Sean McDevitt © Susan Dominus; Introduction to Wolfgang Tillmans © David Deitcher; Introduction to Tony Ward © A.D. Coleman; Introduction to Arthur Tress © Edward Lucie-Smith; all other Introductions © Genevieve Field.

Library of Congress Cataloging-in-Publication Data:
Nerve: the new nude / edited by Genevieve Field.
    p.cm.
ISBN 0-8118-3107-8
        1. Photography of the nude. I. Field, Genevieve.

TR675 .N43 2000
779'.21--dc21

00-025782

Designed by Shawn Hazen
Printed in Hong Kong

Distributed in Canada by Raincoast Books
9050 Shaughnessy Street
Vancouver, British Columbia V6P 6E5

10 9 8 7 6 5 4 3 2 1

Chronicle Books LLC
85 Second Street
San Francisco, California 94105   www.chroniclebooks.com

Cover photo by Leslie Lyons
Back cover photo by Holger Maass

CONTENTS /

What Is *Nerve*?

Introduction

Nerve magazine (www.nerve.com) exists because sex is beautiful and absurd, remarkably fun, and reliably trauma inducing. In short, it's a subject in need of a fearless, intelligent forum for both genders. If you've been looking for a smart, honest magazine on sex, with cliché-shattering prose and striking photographs of naked people that capture more than their flesh, try us.

We welcome your thoughts and feedback on *Nerve* photography at photos@nerve.com.

INTRODUCTION

The body would not be the best-loved subject of generations of artists were its charms not multifarious: it is a palimpsest upon which biographies are written and erased over the course of a lifetime; it is dog-eared and vulnerable; it is honest despite itself; it is a facade; it is a study in geometric abstraction; it is invitingly luminous; it is hard-edged and violent; it is the source of life and a document of erosion; and it is both loved and despised for its elemental sexuality.

Painters and sculptors often acknowledge the importance of trust in the relationship between artist and model, but many photographers go a step farther, believing it to be the essence of a successful picture. Indeed, there is much for the subject to lose when she takes off her clothes (alas, the subject is more often than not female); she is at the mercy of the photographer's whimsy and the viewer's judgment. The photographer, meanwhile, has little to gain without the subject's expressive offerings. A sensitivity to this mutual dependence is what we look for at *Nerve*. Our objective is not only to publish the nude portfolios of the great and up-and-coming photographers but to encourage and cultivate a "new nude"—a photographic approach to the body that is as much about the subject's humanity and sexual character as it is about the photographer's vision.

Some of the photographs collected here pay homage to fine art photography's illustrious canon—from Edward Weston's human landscapes to Imogen Cunningham's ethereal

sprites to Horst's surreal theatrics. But unlike their successors, the old masters of photography largely avoided the sexuality of their subjects by applying the rules of still-life photography to their nudes. The old guard was patient, reverent, and precise—they understood light so well and loved it so resolutely that their first rule might well have been to insist that their models not upstage it. Indeed, one could surmise these masters had little desire to get *under* their subjects' skins. They rejoiced in the human form as a mathematician delights in the irresolvability of pi. Certainly, in their most successful photographs, they also painted a mood: it could be as bright as van Gogh's sunflowers or as sorrowful as Vermeer's empty rooms at dusk, but rarely did it seem to emanate from the subject itself.

Contemporary photographers—many of them entrenched in advertising and fashion—take pictures that reflect an increasingly complicated world. Most seem to have no easy relationship with the beauty that offers itself up to them, which they peel away until imperfections are revealed. From twenty-six-year-old Taryn Simon to sixty-two-year-old Ralph Gibson, the photographers who best represent the editorial direction of *Nerve* read the body by coaxing it out of its standard vocabulary of gestures and poses to express an unscripted history or state of mind. But such insights do not feel stolen or voyeuristic. Again, the empathy between photographer and subject (or photographer and self) offsets a potentially

exploitative dynamic; it is what allows a sexually charged image to transcend the pretentiousness of erotica and the egotism of pornography—genres that serve a more specific, and a less thoughtful, purpose than what we are after with *Nerve* photography.

I am often asked—by devil's advocates, critics, and even some faithful readers—what purpose our photography serves, if not first and foremost to arouse. If we do not fall into the categories of porn or erotica, where do we see ourselves, and why do we focus on nudes at all? Contemplating these questions has helped me to hone my editorial objective and to understand, more clearly with every photograph I view, what it is I am looking for. Our mandate at *Nerve* is to explore the topic of sexuality with all the thoughtfulness it merits. Sex is, after all, a subject of great complexity, and while the body can be an anonymous scrim onto which we humans project our fantasies, *Nerve* is far more interested in how it functions as a vehicle for sexual expression. Our goal, then, is not principally to titillate or to placate the eye, but to explore the myriad ways in which nudity reveals the sexual persona.

In my ideal world, this book would present male and female bodies in equal numbers. The male form, however, has yet to captivate both artists and viewers with the same intensity as the female body. Photographers offer a number of explanations for the discrepancy: women are more accustomed to being gazed upon than men and thus make better subjects; men are less comfortable admiring members of their own sex than women, who often see beauty in both; men are less physically expressive; the male body, some even say, is too overtly sexual. But most strikingly, there seems to be a cultural consensus that women's fantasies are not—or would not be were they given the chance—sparked by visual stimuli to the same degree that men's are. Hence, it may not be overstating the case to say that male homosexual artists are the primary producers of male nudes. This fact presents yet another imbalance—one of "type." While volumes could be—and indeed have been—filled with illustrations of the gay male ideal, selections more varied in appeal, such as those included in this book, are less common. And although the majority of images here depict the female body, it is my hope that this collection, with its type-defying portraits, will intrigue both women and men, gay and straight.

Some of the most surprising and inventive nudes I've seen have been rendered by female artists in their twenties and thirties, many of whom focus on the self-portrait. Unabashedly pointing their lenses at the gritty corners of their own sexual lives, these photographers are upturning—and upstaging—the visual cliché of the passive, fawn-eyed muse. Certainly, more and more images of strong, compelling women are appearing in print advertising as well as in fine art (and perhaps it's no coincidence that the gap between those genres is simultaneously closing). But what can explain the recent much-touted boom in "bad girl" art? Is the sexual revolution only just finding its shape in art? I believe this shift reflects less of a change in how women perceive their sexuality and more of an increase in women's control over how they are perceived.

In the pages that follow, readers will encounter a dramatic range of perceptions—not just of the body, but of race, gender, and sexuality. Because of the difficulty in addressing, in one fell swoop, the breadth of styles and philosophies encompassed by this collection, each photographer's work is accompanied by a short introduction. Not surprisingly, the photographers themselves are best at explaining some of the enigmas of nude photography: why they are compelled to work with nude subjects in the first place, why their models choose to reveal themselves in this most literal of ways, and why the best subject is almost never a professional model. Sylvia Plachy, who photographed ambitious young porn stars in Budapest for *Nerve*, put it best when she said that everybody's armor is different: "For professionals, nudity becomes a clothing. They strike a posture, and it's stylized, it's not them. Who they are I might never see." For most of us, however, undressing necessarily goes hand in hand with letting down our guard—and thus one arrives at the "real people" whose captured images continue to make the nude new.

—Genevieve Field

TARYN SIMON /

Taryn Simon says her self-portraiture, a project that has preoccupied her for the last seven years, is no window into her soul. It began during Simon's freshman year at Brown University, as a way of "entering into the discourse of sexuality and presentation," and soon became her mode of experiencing the world around her. Now, says Simon, "It's transcended that completely. It's much more calculated and private, thus a lot tighter, technically and conceptually." Simon admits to tiring of her affair

with self-portraiture, but she's not yet ready to stop it: "I can't at this point, because it would be a waste of years of work. I do feel somewhat trapped by the whole thing, but the pictures are getting better with my distaste for them."

Indeed, one senses that Simon lives more outside the work than in it. She bares her body; yet her face is a blank slate. Upon it, one viewer may project alienation and ennui; another, tenacity and ambition; still another, sadness.

Simon is a sought-after member of a generation of young photographers who have been accused of ordering style over substance in their work. But Simon is no lightweight; and though often beautiful, her pictures are not easy takes on beauty. In *Narcissus,* she suspends herself over a still lake; reaching tentatively toward the water, she is just on the verge of breaking its surface.

NAN GOLDIN /

The snapshot immediacy of Nan Goldin's photography has become an influential style, but Goldin's real legacy is a history of her times, told in honest portraits of her friends sleeping, bathing, getting high, and making love in the environs of New York City and Europe in the 1980s and '90s.

The intimate nature of Goldin's work can be claustrophobic. She brings viewers into her delicate contract with her subjects, a situation that lifts away the diarist's traditional shroud of privacy. "I started in 1972 long before

Oprah Winfrey-type TV. My motivation was to make the private public because I think the wrong things are kept hidden and hameful, and because revisionism is too widespread n American culture." But invasion is never Goldin's tactic: her photography is about empathy, not voyeurism.

These days, the word *sentimental* is used almost exclusively as a pejorative, but Goldin reinvests sentiment with its full, Romantic meaning; emotion overwhelms intellectual ideology. Much of her mature work

has documented the impact of AIDS on her and her friends' lives, hitting the viewer with a powerful emotional wallop. But in recent years, Goldin has mellowed; her rage and rebellion have given way to a maturation born from seasoned experiences of intense love, loss, and mourning. In these images, she seems to vacillate between aging gracefully and maintaining the abandonment of youth.

SYLVIA PLACHY /

A Sylvia Plachy photo is rarely perfect. The horizon may be slightly off-kilter, the point of focus resting just beyond the subject's face, the sky a bright whitewash. Yet rather than distract, these minor technical imperfections beckon; like a beautiful face with crooked features, a signature Plachy image hovers somewhere between exotic and earthly. In her translation, while the most uncommon subject is demystified, the most banal may find eloquence.

Plachy is a seasoned documentary photographer; her professional career began in college when she sold *Confrontation,* a photograph of her husband and father arguing, to the Museum of Modern Art. Since then, Plachy has moved easily among military zones, urban jungles, and red-light districts. Her first foray into the sex industry, to make the book *Red Light* with journalist James Ridgeway, was daunting. Plachy was initially disturbed by the

"downward, self-destructive bend many of the people were taking." Yet in the strange environs of brothels, strip clubs, and porn sets, she found some of her most "vital, energetic, funny, and interesting" subjects to date.

Some years after completing *Red Light,* Plachy returned to the sexual underground to photograph the players in Budapest's emerging porn industry for *Nerve.* While there, she fell in love with Martina, a Laura Dern look-alike

whose career in porn had propelled her out of poverty. "There's always someone who will captivate me more than others," Plachy says. "Martina's courage captivated me. She was hell-bent on being a star; she was quite an exhibitionist, and it's ideal for a photographer to have someone who wants to be photographed. Still, as nice as she and the others were, I couldn't believe they were doing this without any protection—no condoms, nothing. I don't like looking at things like that, because I know what the risks are." Yet Plachy, it seems, would never bother to shoot nudes in a neutral setting: "When a body is just used as a geometric representation it's not as interesting. I like things that are more emotional."

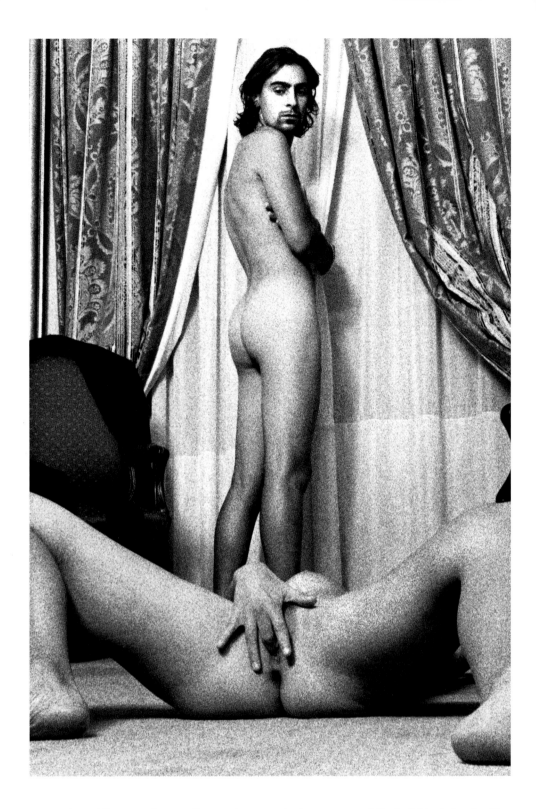

TONY WARD /

Physicists speak of perturbation, the ineluctable fact that the act of observation changes the situation observed. The people in these pictures are not fashion models posing on a shoot; and these images do not capture "found" moments either. Ward didn't require his subjects to do what they do here, nor did he entice them to act in ways they wouldn't have behaved on their own. Rather, they sought him out, convinced him to help them stage and commemorate their fantasies and fetishes, and invited him to cross the

proscenium of these erotic narratives and become both dramaturge and unseen actor. The challenge, accepted and met by Ward, was that of entering into and enhancing the spirit of the proceedings so as to understand and represent them as a form of performance art.

What does it feel like to watch sex from a participant's vantage? What are the visual moments in the flux and strain of sexual ritual and erotic abandon that, transmuted into silver particles and then into ink on paper, can transmit some of that energy to someone

who knows none of the individuals involved? When and how do you transcend your self-consciousness before the stare of the camera and either forget it's there or look it square in the eye? How can lens and film, at the command of a keen and empathetic visual intelligence, register some of that vitality? These are the kinds of questions that Tony Ward's inquisitive, empathetic, amoral imagery both asks and answers.

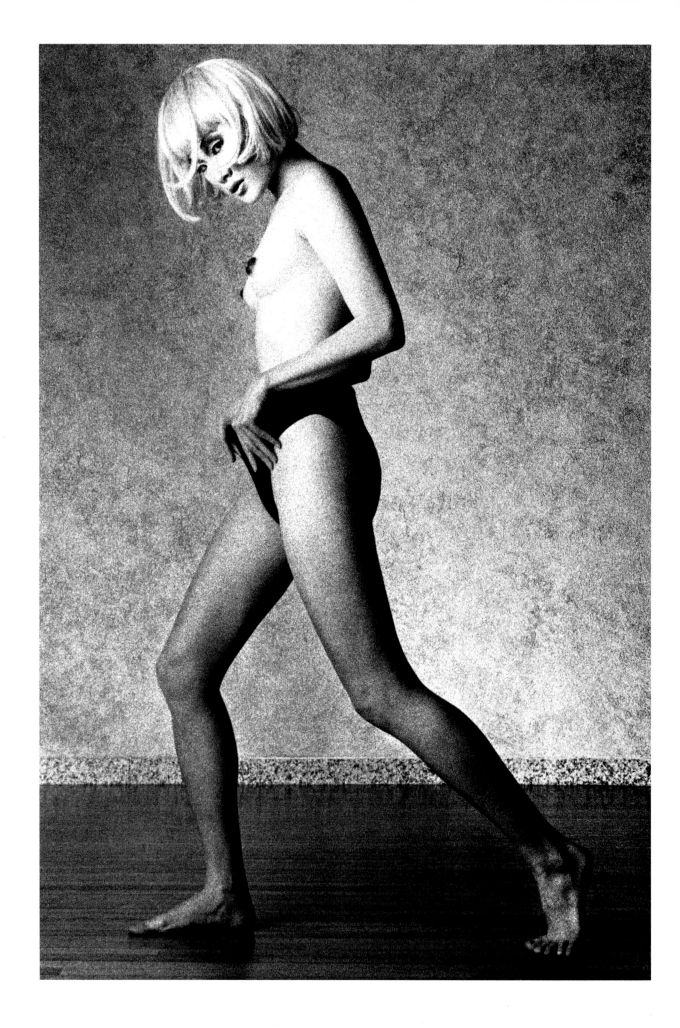

RICHARD KERN /

Richard Kern is best known for his brutally sordid films (*Fingered, Zombie Hunger*, and so on) and for his noir-inspired photographs of predatory women who look like they have a taste for pain—perhaps *your* pain. For years, Kern shot bad girls in his East Village apartment, developing a body of work marked by candy-colored backdrops, aggressively attractive models, and a lot of ropes and latex.

Kern's most recent work has taken a turn. The bolt holes in the doorways have been spackled over, and the curtains are open; gone

are the grunge-babes lounging on tacky futons, ornamented with dripping candles and sundry piercings. In their stead, ethereal women— many of them fans whom Kern travels to Europe to photograph—parade around sun-blanched kitchens and bathrooms like streaking Vanna Whites. And then there are the men—who are surlier than the women, albeit, but just as fresh. Kern says the new look is about "trying to give justification to a picture of someone with their clothes off so that it's more than a pretty picture." Though

they *are* pretty, Clorox-bright portraits like these of *Marissa* and *Tracy* mark an important shift for Kern—his acknowledgment that sometimes softer is stronger.

GREG FRIEDLER /

There is a certain hard-to-pin-down quality possessed by the women in these photographs: something ethereal, yet utterly grounded—for lack of a better way to describe the confluence, something spiritual. Greg Friedler, the young photographer known for his *Naked New York, Naked Los Angeles,* and *Naked London* books, seems to get closer, every year of his career, to his ambition: "I keep wanting to discover more, something deeper and more pure," he explains. "It really doesn't have much to do with sexuality. I still think bodies are these weird things—

they're made beautiful in a picture when there's eye contact." Indeed, it's impossible to study the bodies of these models-next-door without feeling engaged in a visual dialogue. The viewer must meet their gaze or look away.

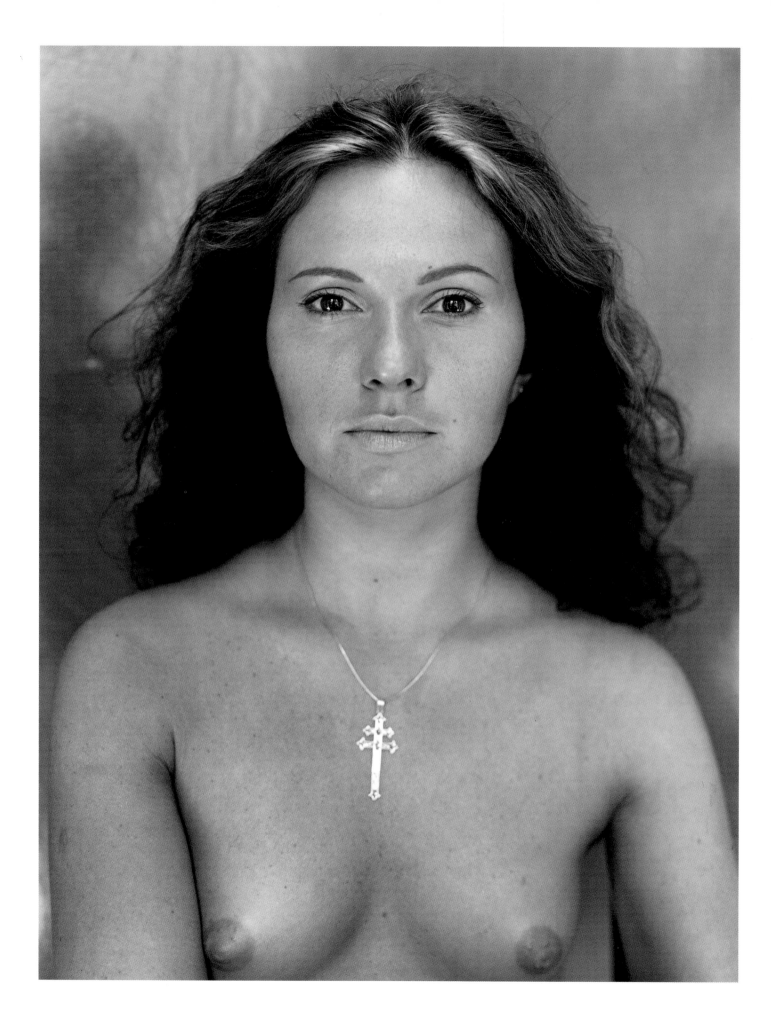

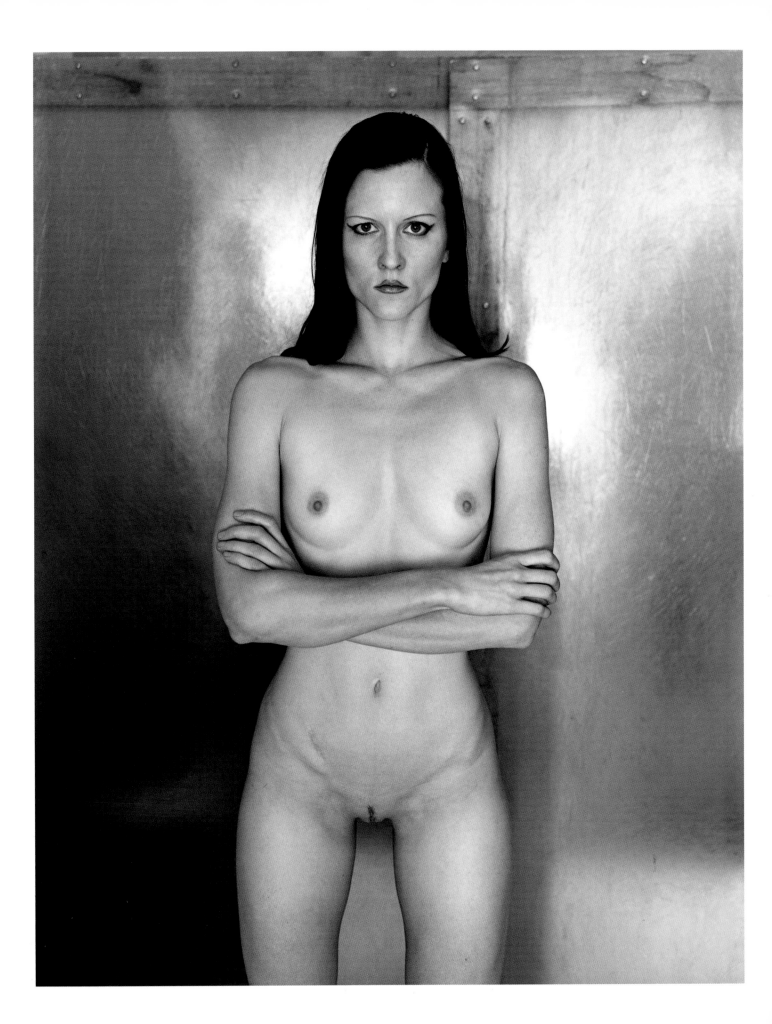

ROBERT STIVERS /

Unlike most of us, Robert Stivers seems to enjoy poking around in the dark nether regions of his mind, where phantom memories lurk, occasionally swimming close to the surface like luminous fish. Stivers traps those slippery impressions but does not try to explain them: "I love ambiguity in my art," he says, "but I'm always searching for meaning in my personal life." That search began when an injury removed Stivers' greatest passion—dance—from his repertoire. No longer able to express himself through movement, he wan-dered for a while through jobs as an arts administrator, financial planner, and photogra-phers' agent before "coming back to my heart" and taking up dance choreography and photography. He began performing again, too—in art galleries instead of onstage. In one performance piece, Stivers writhed in a straitjacket before a Super-8 image of a baby crying, to the music of Vivaldi. Emotional violence runs rampant under a thin veneer of tranquility in all of his work. His faceless—sometimes headless—figures inhabit their sur-roundings with a ghostly absence that con-notes the photographer's own heartache.

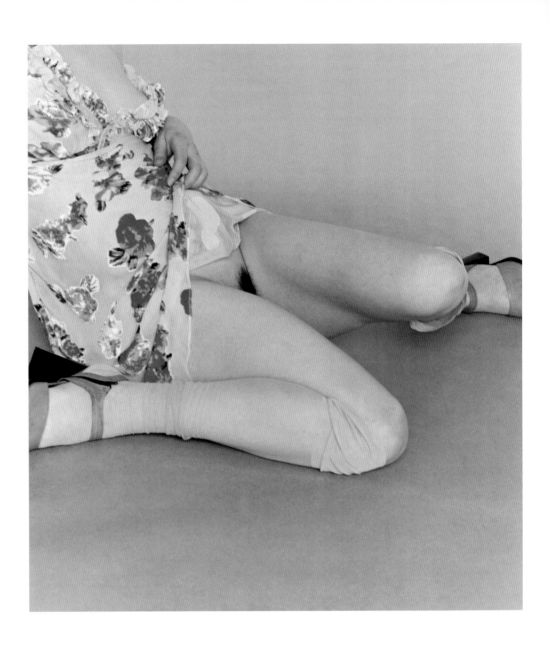

LESLIE LYONS /

How Leslie Lyons chooses her subjects is as inexplicable to her as the artistic process itself: she might pass a young woman on a city street, exchange a quick, almost accidental glance, and know with surprising certainty that she's found her next model. Whether she intends to re-create the dreamy, loose-limbed subjects sketched by the fin-de-siècle artist Egon Schiele or to depict a memorably exuberant cartoon character drawn by comic book artist David Mack, Lyons relies more on instinct than on a surface appraisal in approaching potential models. She had no reason to guess that the young, conservatively dressed Asian-American woman pictured on the following pages would agree to collaborate with her on the Mack-inspired photographs: "How I knew is a complete mystery," she says, "and I hope I never find out."

In photographing nudes, Lyons says she's challenged herself in a way that translates into more articulate images, regardless of the subject. "Now that I've endeavored to discover those private aspects of myself and of my models," she says, "I find there's that inclination to try to reveal something deeper, something hidden in every image I capture on camera."

IAN MCFARLANE /

The warm Georgia light illuminating many of Ian McFarlane's quiet photographs is just one aspect of the work that bespeaks his native South. One senses that these pictures weren't taken in a hurry. When he's not photographing himself, McFarlane usually works with good friends who, he says, are endlessly accommodating of his slow process. Twenty-four shots can require a two-hour sitting, during which the models find a pose and hold it, waiting for the light to shift across their bodies. "My photographs are very southern, but that's all I know," he says.

McFarlane's humility is manifest in all his work, from the three self-portraits shown here to the lonely, simple image of a woman half-undressed before a smoking campfire. When asked about the lack of "edge" to his work, he replies: "Edge is when people have too much of a preconceived idea of what they want to create and don't just let themselves go and find out what can come of something that doesn't exist yet. When you don't give up control you have edge. There's no realness, no romance, no humanity to it."

McFarlane's artistic philosophy echoes that of his favorite master, Henri Cartier-Bresson, who said: "A photograph is neither taken nor seized by force. It offers itself up. It is the photo that takes you. One must not take photos."

CAMELLA GRACE /

Camella Grace was a sexual late bloomer. "There wasn't a lot out there to feed and nurture me as a woman," she says. "Nothing spoke to me." For Grace, sex was anti-climactic, and porn was one-sided. So she began rummaging through her subconscious for fantasies she could call her own, holding on to the images that flashed behind her eyelids during moments of arousal.

In her search for a sexual outlet, Grace became an exotic dancer. It was a short-lived experience. "While the women I met were empowered by the industry, most of them were victims of sexual abuse and were in bad relationships," says Grace. "It seemed weird to me that what should be the perfect place to express oneself is just a manifestation of bad attitudes about women and sex."

Compelled to claim and map the uncharted territories of female sexuality for herself and her friends, Grace turned to photography. "I left the world of what I thought everything was supposed to be, trying to transcend traditional human experience as much as possible. And I realized that I have some crazy fantasies." But perhaps her images of groping arms, shadowy faces, and black-kohled eyes aren't so much crazy as they are eerily familiar.

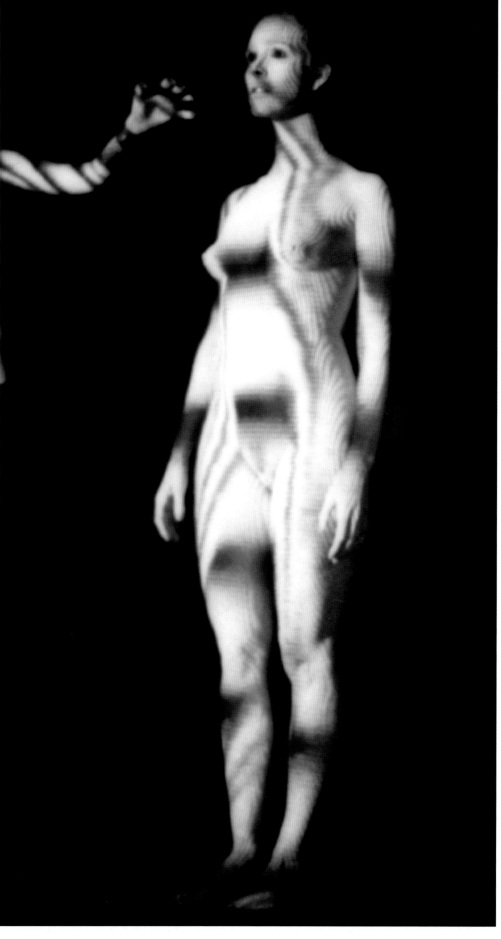

THOMAS CARABASI /

One might guess that Thomas Carabasi recruited his models from a local dance studio—their long limbs and graceful movements all suggest time spent in front of mirrored walls and ballet bars. Carabasi did choreograph their moves, predetermining where the arrow on the Twister wheel would fall, but his subjects were actually fellow artists, photographers, and painters who volunteered to be models for his human sculptures.

Once poised, they were lit from a single source, their bodies frozen by a strobe into white stone. The resulting compositions are Carabasi's tribute to centuries-old figure studies in which "the nude" was not limited to a solitary form. "I wanted to combine the realism of photography with the content of classical painting and drawing," he says, "placing emphasis on the mythical and the metaphorical rather than on the formal."

The communal nudes of the Renaissance, the crowded arrangements and chiaroscuro of Mannerism, and the order and idealization of seventeenth-century French classical painting all meld together in the limbs of Carabasi's subjects, creating a complex puzzle that the eye happily struggles to solve.

MARCELO KRASILCIC /

Marcelo Krasilcic's greatest inspirations are pornography and soap operas. "From soaps I take the drama of evil and good," he says. And from porn, one surmises, he takes a full-blooded appreciation for sex. Born in Brazil, Krasilcic learned early on how to embrace pleasure, but he says his Jewish faith instilled in him reflexes he can't quite shirk. "Largely, my photography is about not wanting to feel guilty," he admits.

Though photographing men "relates more to [his] sexuality," Krasilcic's women are equally seductive. In this series, which he calls "a dialogue between humans and the divine," Krasilcic is at his most graceful. Curtains fall like the softest hair, and a cold expanse of wood floor is inviting. "There is something poetic about how someone sets up a room," he says. "It's a delicate, clear intention—a balance between the person and the world they created." Which is more "beautiful" for Krasilcic, one wonders—a body or a chair? No matter: in his eyes, it's all exposed, vulnerable, and beautiful.

PLATE: **042**

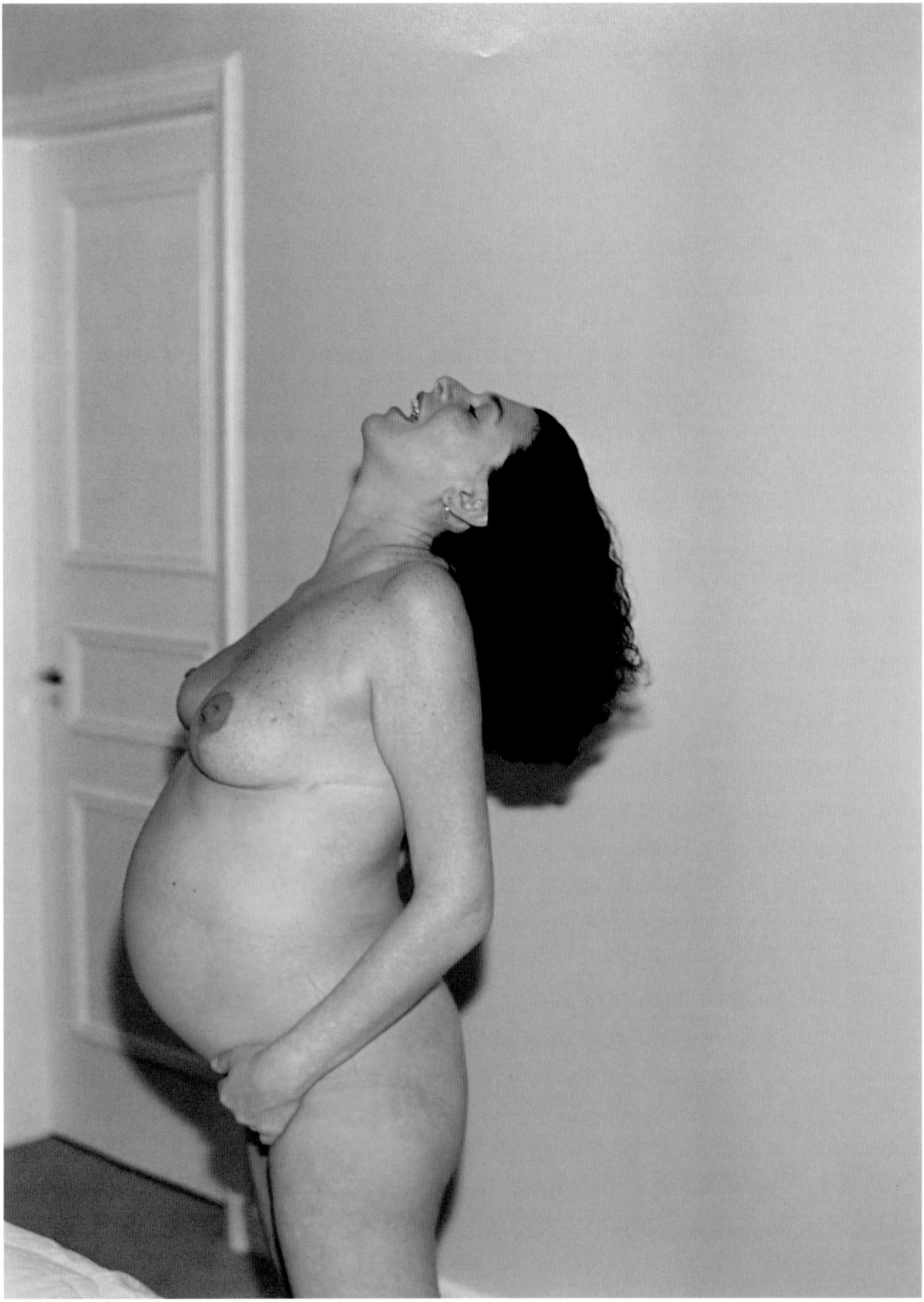

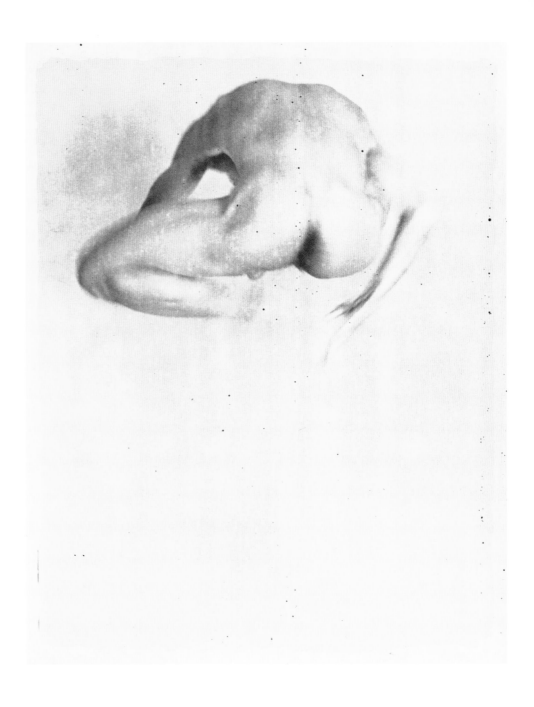

ALVIN BOOTH /

It seems fitting that Alvin Booth's studio is not the white-walled, sun-washed void that one sees in movies about New York photographers, that the artist's workspace should be as atavistic as the images he painstakingly constructs. Booth works and lives with his wife and collaborator, Nike, on the third floor of a creaky Manhattan brownstone. Heavy velvet drapes hang in paned-glass windows, and Rachmaninoff concertos swell throughout the long afternoons that Booth spends sewing his models' costumes—corsets, skirts,

and harnesslike contraptions—from membranous latex. The models, handpicked as much for their patience and good humor as for their sinuous physiques, are painted gold or occasionally dusted with talcum powder. Then, leaping, twisting, and contorting, they transform Booth's book-cramped living room into an otherworldly dance atelier.

While many photographers work with nude models to escape the time-and-date imprimatur of fashion, few are able to completely shake the aesthetic of their day. Booth succeeds in

doing so not by eradicating all cultural referents but by calling upon his favorites from the past and future: the constrained eroticism of Victorian pornography, the exhibitionism of modern fetishism, and the *Bladerunner*esque survivalism of a science fiction dystopia all collude in these pictures, leaving the viewer unsure whether to feel tugged forward or backward in time.

ROBERT MAXWELL /

Though he makes a living shooting hipster celebrity portraits for glossies like *Vanity Fair* and *Vibe*, Robert Maxwell has stopped reading magazines altogether for fear of being influenced by his peers. Although he's living in a digital age, the photographs closest to his heart could come from another era. "Ten years from now I don't want people to say, 'Oh, that was in 1990. And that was in 1980,'" he says. "If you can immediately date it, it's not a good photograph." Maxwell is one of the few photographers today making

ambrotypes—a process reminiscent of the nineteenth-century collodion wet-plate technique. It's a painstaking art: Maxwell spends the night before a photo shoot hand polishing sheets of glass that will serve as his negatives. On the day of the session, he coats the sheets with a collodion solution, then dips them in a bath of silver nitrate. When he removes the plate, it's light sensitive, and Maxwell immediately attaches it to his camera, removing the lens cap to make the exposure. He has three minutes to take the pic-

ture before the plate starts to dry. On a good day Maxwell will take just twenty frames, giving himself enough room to select one or two powerful, but never perfect, images. Only recently has he pushed his nudes into a more sexual realm. "I've always wanted to approach things that the masses would call pornographic or lewd or dirty and find the beauty in them," he says.

SEAN MCDEVITT /

Sean McDevitt, a mild-mannered twenty-nine-year-old guy in a baseball cap and a flannel shirt, makes a very unconvincing exhibitionist. Yet McDevitt is both artist and exhibitionist, a photographer who invites the public, colleagues, and, on occasion, his own mother to peer at images of him wearing lacy garters, jacking off in the sink, or thrusting his ass at the camera lens. Although he considers the portraits he does of others to be his best work, some of his most powerful photographs are of himself as he displays his fetish for women's lingerie.

McDevitt takes these pictures for the same reason he started stealing his mother's silky underwear when he was about eleven: he liked the way it felt. It got him off. "Part of the fantasy, part of the excitement, is getting caught," says McDevitt. "I'm my own voyeur. I catch myself, on camera."

The pictures have functioned, he admits, both as self-expression and as personal advertisement. Most of the women he's dated have approached him after seeing his work and finding it exciting. McDevitt's current girlfriend is the exception (they met through other channels), but she is enthusiastic about his work. "She's very pretty in a feminine way," he says. "I love women's bodies. I dress up to turn myself on by looking like one. But I'm also attracted to women who look like men. And I like penises. A beautiful woman with a penis—that would be ideal."

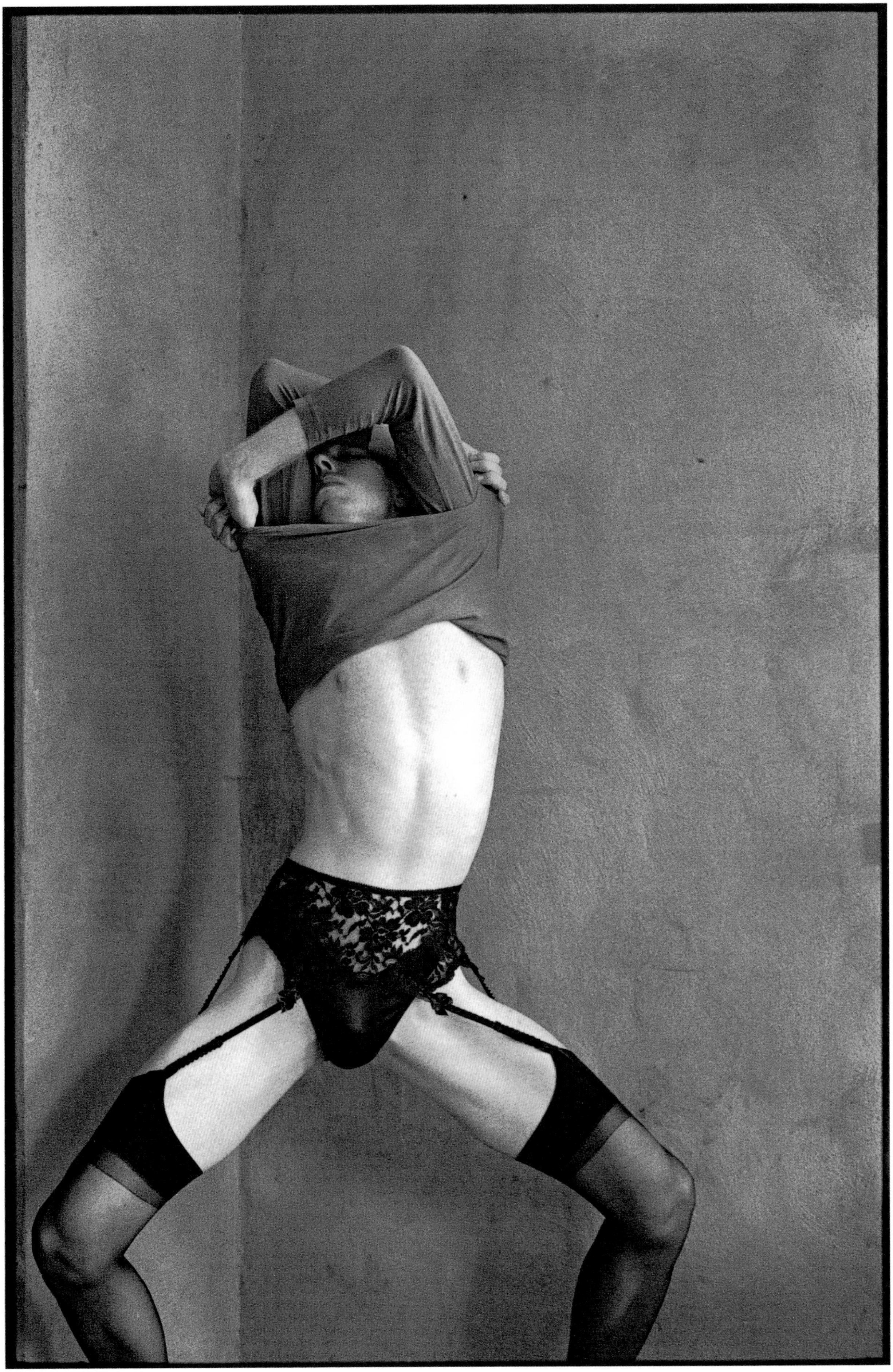

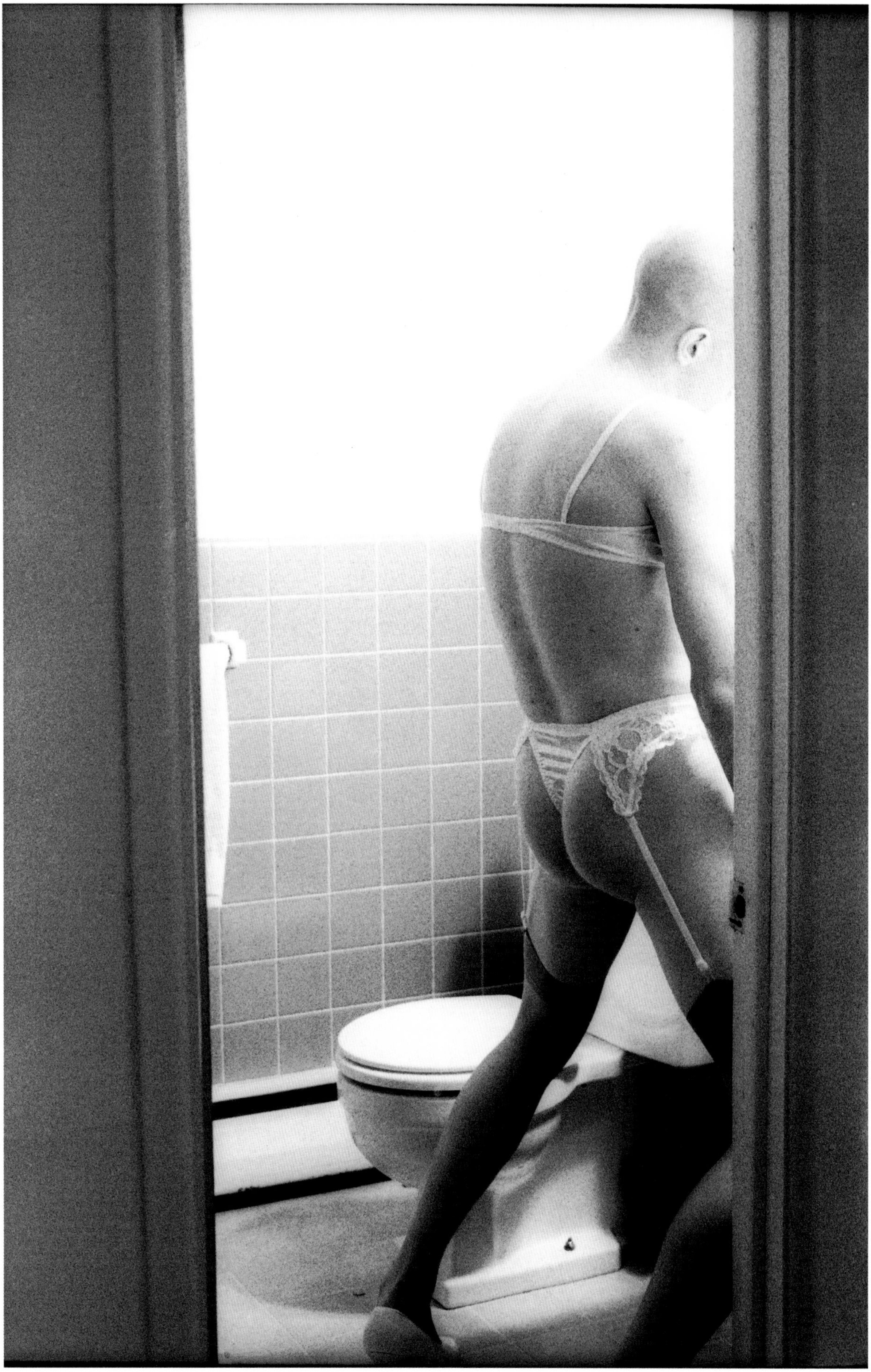

RENEE COX /

Pointing to the larger-than-life-sized nude hanging in her living room, Renee Cox says, "You see, I wasn't supposed to look like that after having a child. I was supposed to have crawled up somewhere and died. . . . But," she adds, tossing her meticulously groomed dreadlocks, "as you can see the body is tight. The pumps are on. And I'm ready to do my shit and look good doing it."

The photograph, entitled *Yo Mama,* depicts Cox, naked except for heels, holding her young child with a firmly loving grip. One of Cox's alter egos (and a distant psychic cousin of Rajé, Cox's fifty-foot superhero), *Yo Mama* states very confidently that she wants and deserves to be seen. Her self-possession—caught as she is in her own gaze—is almost a challenge, as if she defies the viewer to deny her any aspect of her multifaceted femininity. Cox's work forces us to create new categories, to accept that art can be both a resolute statement and an elegant embrace of form.

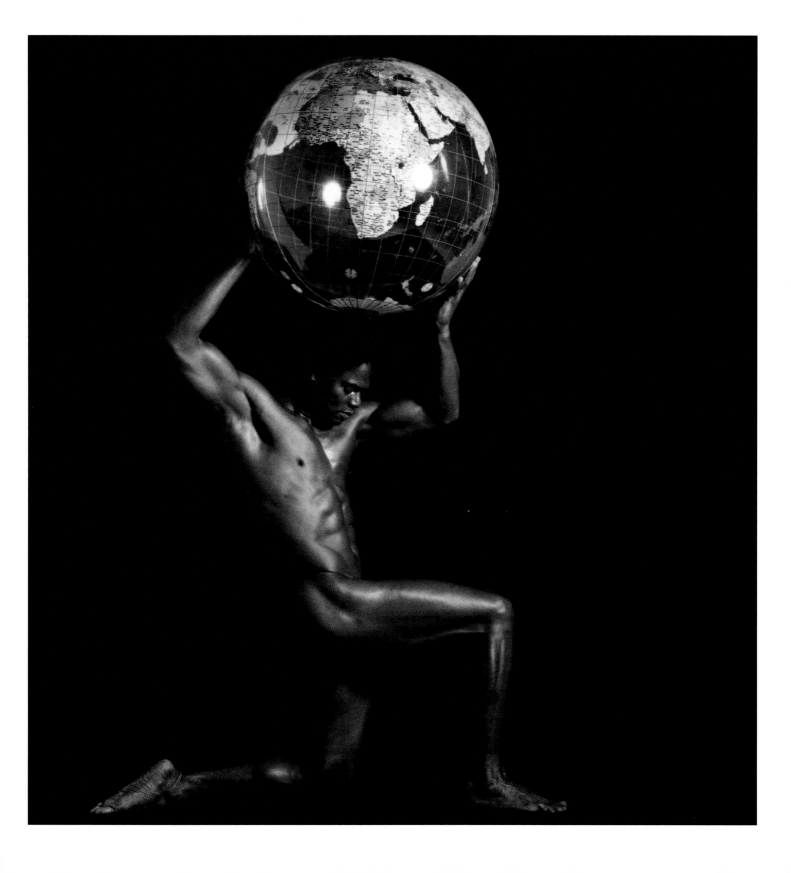

TERRY RICHARDSON /

Terry Richardson is a fashion photographer with the sense of humor to take the industry with a grain of salt. Fashion work is fine with Richardson, because it pays good money, the women are beautiful, and, for him, it's *easy*. But what he actually prefers is real life.

Richardson, whose father is the once-celebrated fashion photographer Bob Richardson, first picked up a camera at age sixteen, but he put it down shortly thereafter, discouraged by his dad's lack of enthusiasm for the work. Seven years later, while living in New York's East Village, the younger Richardson decided that life was too messy an event not to capture it on film. The pictures he took there—sexy, gutsy, gauche—drew the attention of designer Katharine Hamnett, who hired Richardson for her new campaign. Richardson was soon challenging the industry's notion of glamor with gritty, not-so-pretty realism in editorials for *Vogue* and *Elle*. (Perhaps one is less fearful of rendering Kate Moss gritty if he's been raised among celebrities: Richardson's parents split when he was four; his dad took up with a very young Anjelica Huston and his mom with Jimi Hendrix.)

While some critics complain that Richardson tries too hard to maintain his bad-boy credentials (a 1999 gallery exhibit featured numerous photographs of shit and of private parts both human and feline), he's widely loved for photographs like the ones shown here—sometimes straightforward, sometimes whimsical, always honest to a forgivable fault.

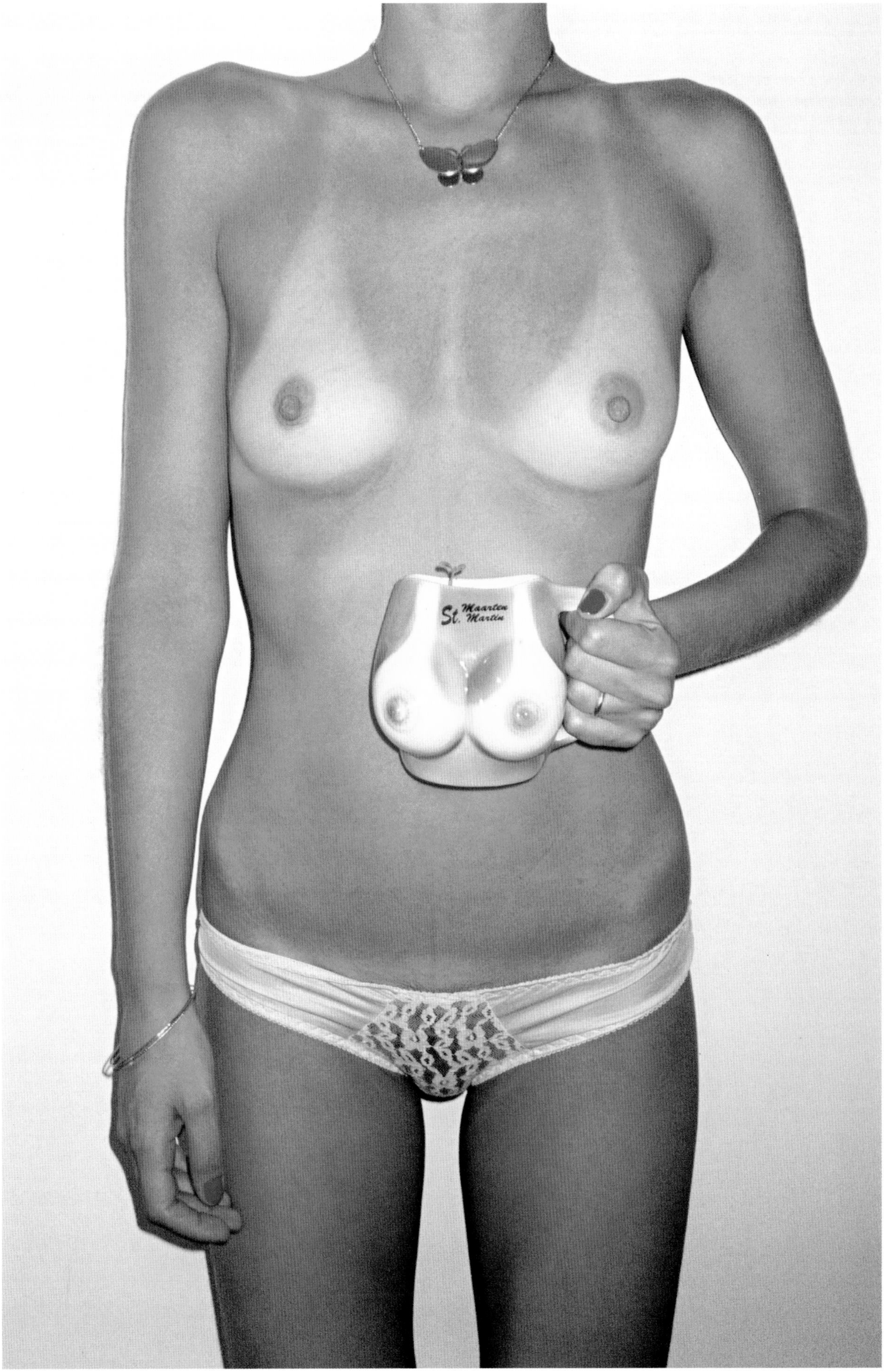
St. Maarten
Martin

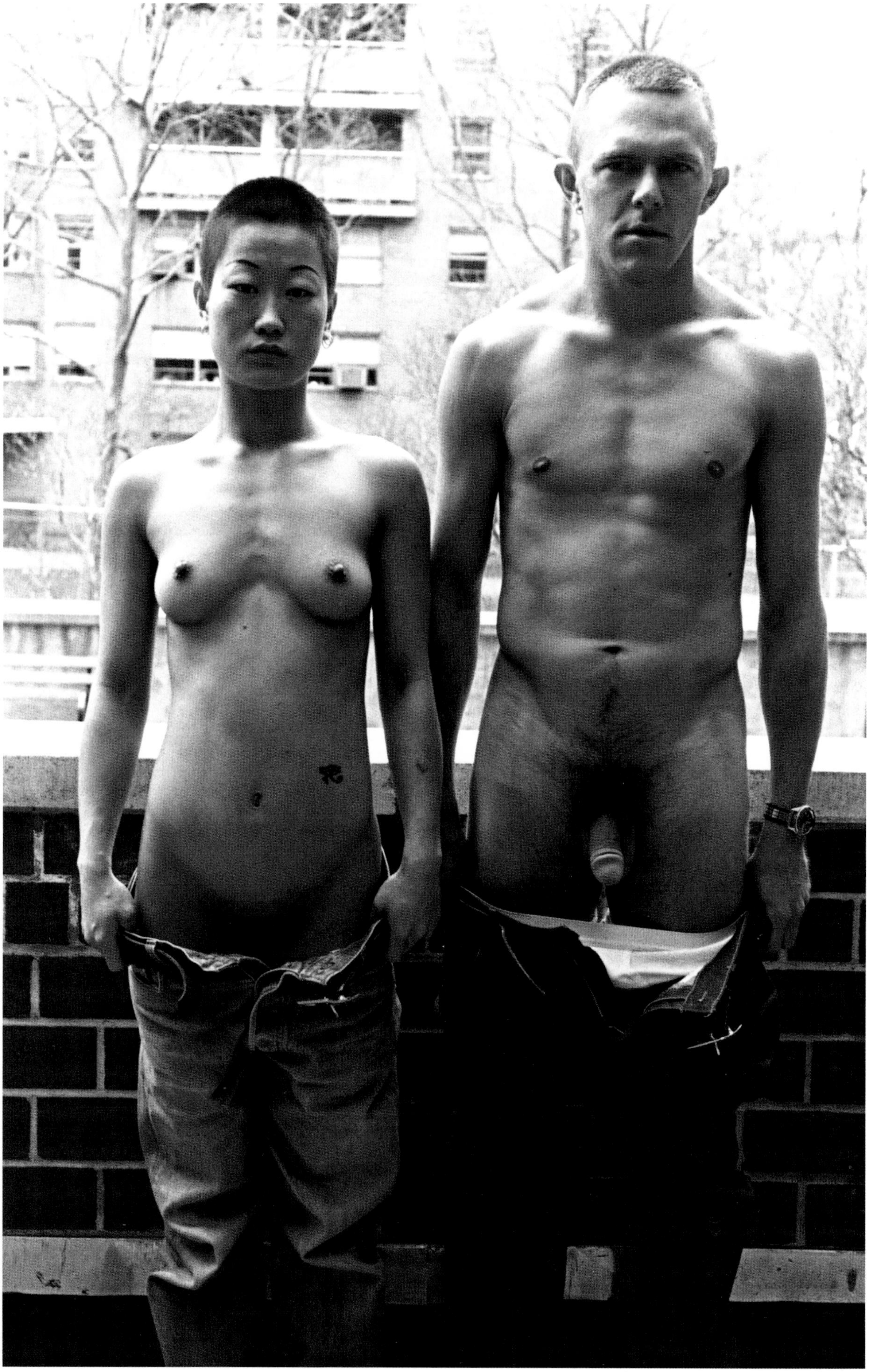

ARTHUR TRESS /

Arthur Tress has always been obsessed with the image of the male—male beauty, male potency, sometimes male terror. In a sense, he has been fortunate in his time, which has witnessed an extraordinary change of attitudes toward representations of the male nude. Not so long ago—in fact until the very end of the 1960s—such representations were more or less outlawed. Now, with gay liberation and the continuing rise of feminism, they have become less questionable than equivalent images of females. While a female nude imme-

diately raises the complex politics of gender— of who looks, and with what motivation in mind—a male nude doesn't evoke centuries of subjection.

Tress' nudes are deeply romantic—in spirit, not merely in style. His work has always dealt not simply in images as such, but in metaphors and symbols, treated in the expansive, open-ended way of the Romantic poetry of the nineteenth century.

In this sense, Tress is true to photography's Victorian roots. The Victorians discovered

that one of the unexpected strengths of the photographic image was its ability to capture both the sharp particularity of dreams and the sense of remove that the dreamer often experiences.

CHARLES GATEWOOD /

When Charles Gatewood began documenting the sexual underground in the mid-'60s, tattooing, piercing, exhibitionism, and gender bending were barely a blip on the radar screen of most Americans. That was before models accentuated their rib cages with dresses held together by rows of giant safety pins, before tattoos came to symbolize the rite of passage from childhood to adulthood, and before tourists paid to be spanked in public at S/M-theme restaurants. Now Gatewood's subjects are not so much freaks as they are countercultural icons.

Gatewood has been called a prophet, a revolutionary, and the "direct photographic descendant" of the famous photo-documentarian Weegee. A schooled anthropologist, he is naturally curious about aberrant cultures; a nonconformist himself, he is always willing to "join in the dance," the better to understand his subjects: "Are there still areas of the behavioral map marked *unknown*?" he asks. "If so, book my passage at once."

HIROSHI SUNAIRI /

Hiroshi Sunairi is a narcissist who is saved by his sense of humor. In lieu of the obligatory "artist's statement" that accompanies, but rarely illuminates, most gallery exhibitions, one from a Sunairi show will read like this: "Dig a hole, put a seed in it, pour some water, wait till it grows, dance around it, stamp around it, put some nuts around it, let the sun shine on it, pray, tell yourself, feed yourself, tell other people about it, let them grow it, let them say it their way."

A fixture in the New York performance art community, one of Sunairi's best-known pieces is "Early-Hiroshi Television," a thirteen-minute video featuring Sunairi masturbating. In the context of an art gallery, such work is meant to negate its own eroticism, but Sunairi doesn't shy away from traditional porn venues. One piece of art that was most likely taken at face value by its primary audience was a spread of graphic self-portraits he published in *Playguy* magazine. "I like the idea that readers are becoming a voyeur of me," he told *i-D* magazine for an article on new trends in photography called "Constant Stiffies." "I look at them while they look at me—in doing this, I am also a voyeur. The fact that I can make art in the pornographic context is interesting to me."

Yet as much as he exerts irreverence and a pop sensibility, Sunairi's romantic alter ego comes out in some of his best work. *Hiroshima, Pour Bonne Nuit (by window)* is his most delicate photograph; in it Sunairi reclines by a lace-curtained window, bathed in dappled blue light.

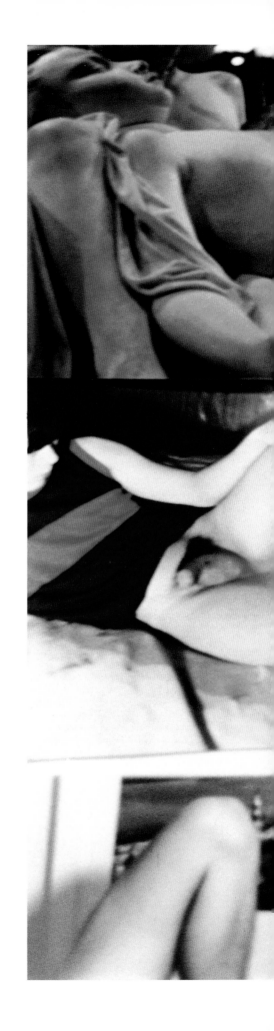

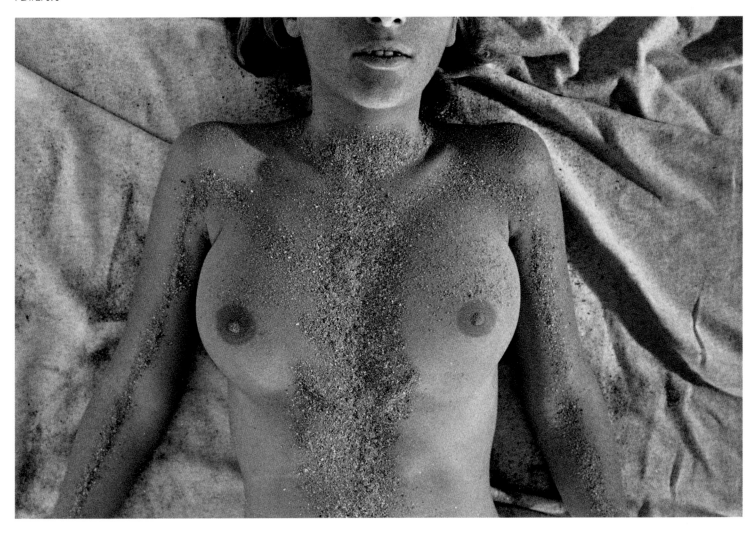

FRÉDÉRIC GOUDAL (FiLH) /

Frédéric Goudal hates seduction. "Active seduction is about faking somebody out, it's about entrapment. There are those who tend to dislike my work because my models aren't 'seductive' enough. But I don't want people to enjoy my photography simply because there's a good-looking woman staring back at them." While Goudal may be more interested in documenting the natural female form than in idealizing his subject, the form he photographs is more in his element than hers. He admits, "When a model comes in front

of my camera, I consider her to be an actor; she's playing a role. I wouldn't presume to capture her personality."

Instead, he creates what he calls a "naked journey" from the academic (mirrors multiplying and fragmenting the body) to the abstract (various textiles producing second surfaces of skin). On that journey, Goudal has favorite landmarks—cropped torsos, buoyant derrieres, bodies in repose. Goudal approaches these landmarks from a different direction with each series but is not the least bit concerned with

appearing erratic. He concludes, "I'd rather be incoherent than boring."

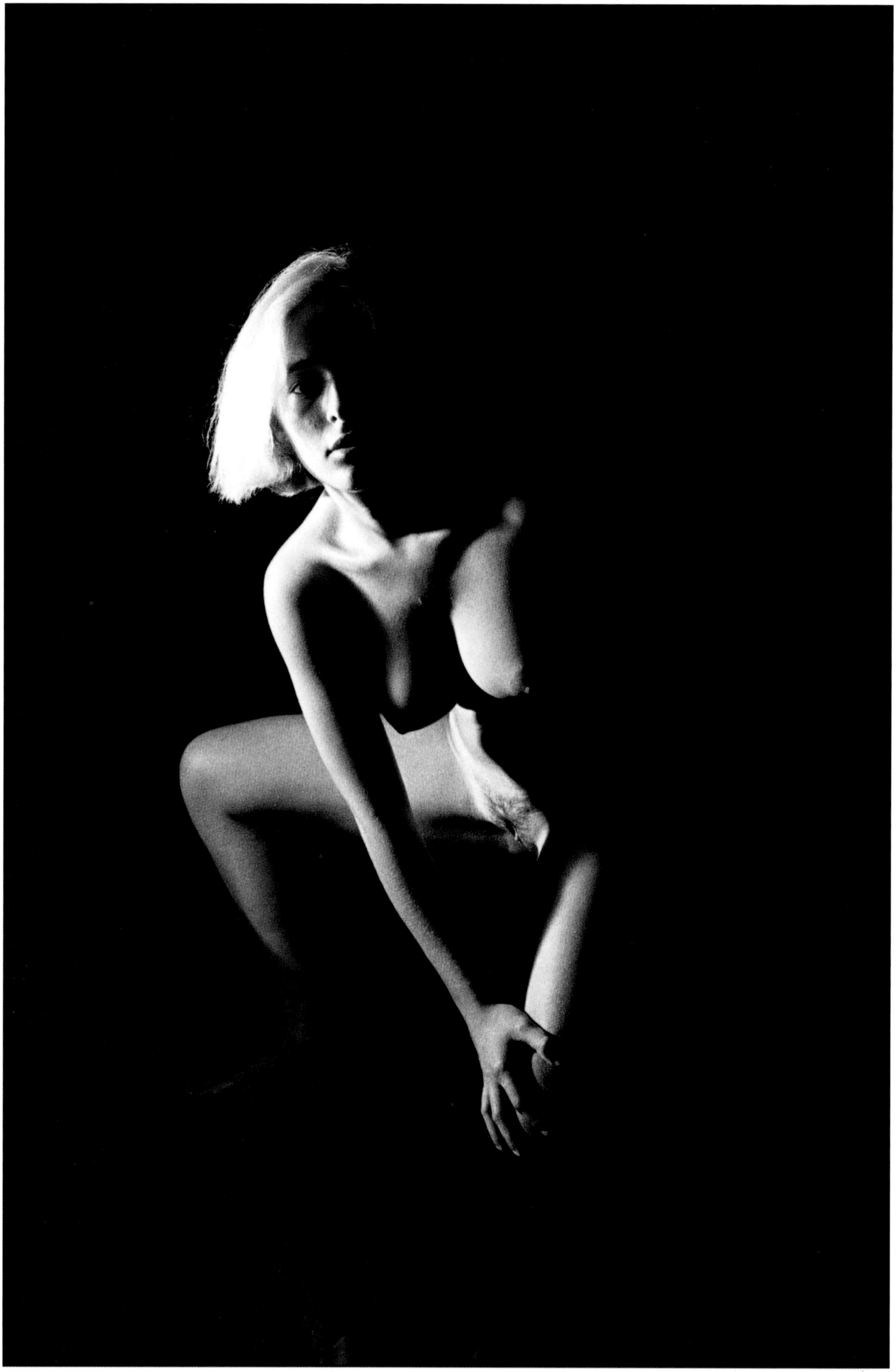

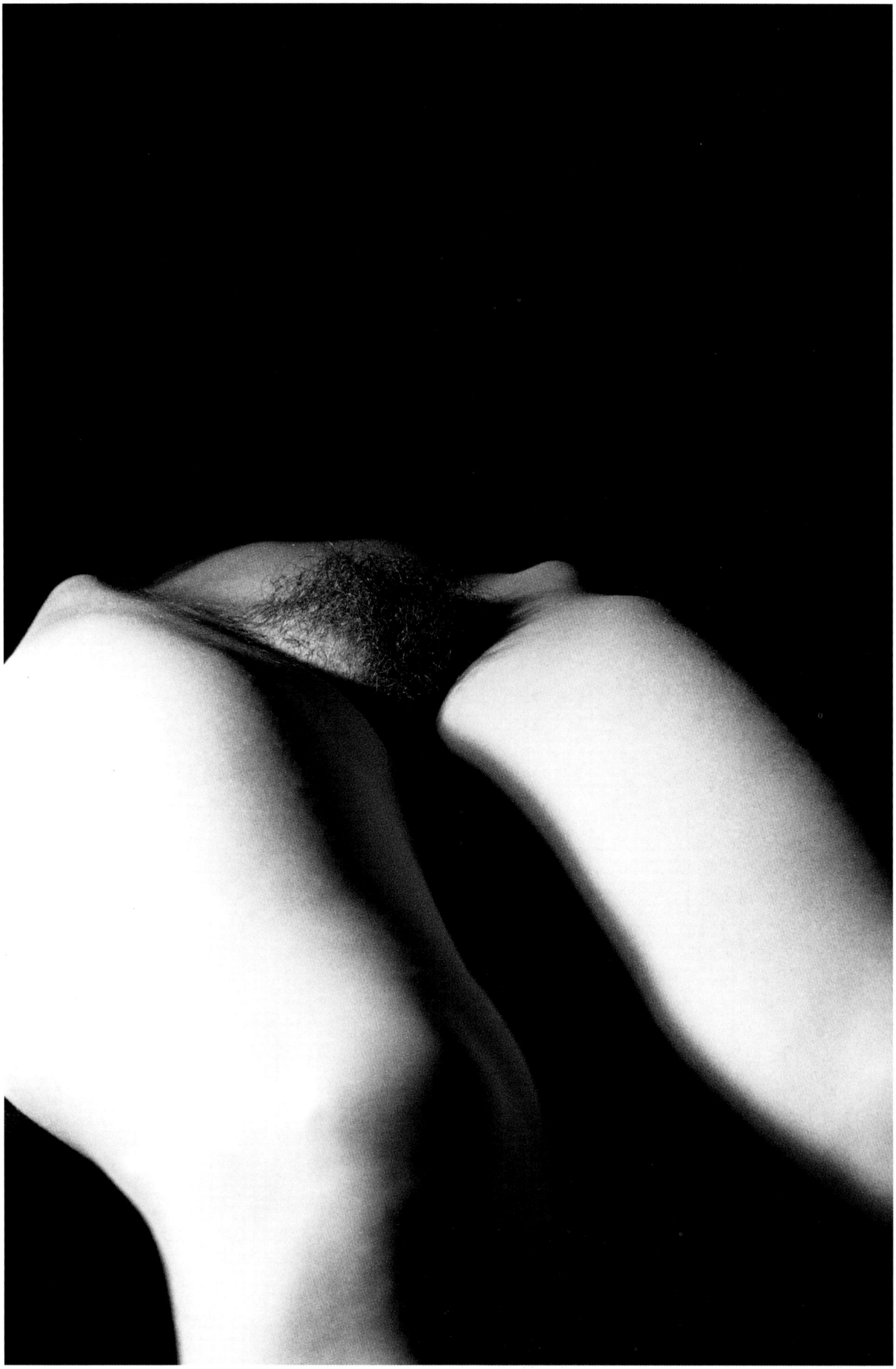

JESSICA CRAIG-MARTIN /

Jessica Craig-Martin's career among the paparazzi began when Anna Wintour offered her a job shooting parties for *Vogue* magazine. During the three years since that meeting, the photographer has been thrown into a wide range of situations that sometimes fit only loosely under the heading of "party." She's found that it's possible to capture the images that *Vogue* needs while taking another series of pictures just to the left and right of the fiction that glamor seeks. Of course, when things stop being perfect, they get a lot

more interesting: "The experience highlighted in these pictures is an orgy that took place on a boat after the Venice Bienale. Speeding across open water toward the outer islands, I noticed bits of clothing being offered to the waves. Before long everyone seemed to be fondling, sucking, or licking something. The genitalia of strangers doesn't interest me that much, but I did have my camera with me, so I wasn't at all bored.

"The sex flared up and died down in waves throughout the night, punctuated by outbursts

of violence. Finally, the exhausted revelers lay strewn like dead birds around the cabin. I sat on the steps of the boat, contemplating the beauty of the city gliding toward us. The atmosphere of soul rot was palpable, but at least the sex had stopped for good. Or had it? I felt something stroking my cheek—looked to my left—there, parallel with my face, was an erect penis. I turned back to Venice. Oh, I thought. Just another cock."

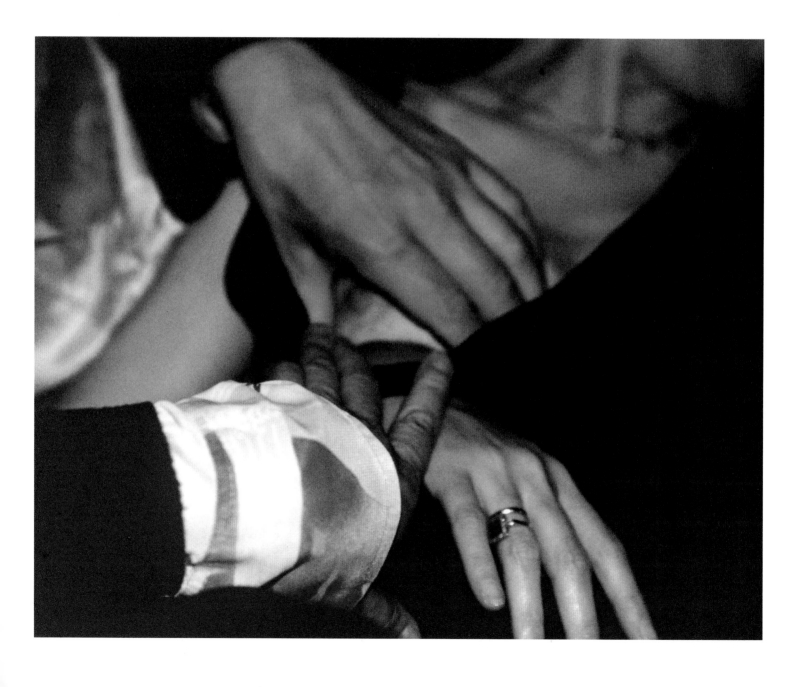

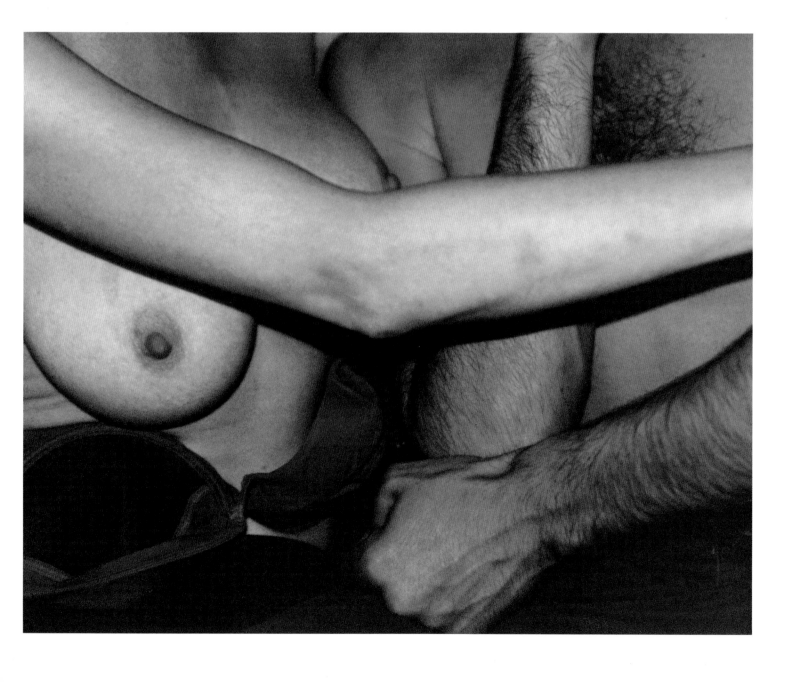

THOMAS KARSTEN /

Thomas Karsten's subjects vary not only in their sexual preferences but also in their choices of physical space. Some, looking for a lark, insist on being photographed in foreign environments. "They want to escape from ordinary life and express their usually subdued sexual wishes and ideas." Others feel secure in their homes where beds, bathtubs, and armchairs are reassuring yet, in the context of nude portraiture, patently sexual. Still others prefer to have their pictures taken out of doors—acting, perhaps, on some primordial

urge to streak. "Unfortunately," rues the German-based Karsten, "I don't live in California."

Karsten's models decide not only the *where,* but the *what:* "They reveal things that they've never revealed before, not even to their partners. Once a model spontaneously wrote some words on her body with lipstick, among them the phrase 'love me.' This got me thinking: every woman, indeed every human, wants to be loved the way she is. The women in my photographs present themselves in the

way they want to be loved." Baring all for the camera may not be the most effective way to get love, but Karsten's work—sharp, honest, respectful—suggests it may be the most honest.

VALERIE GALLOWAY /

"I'm sweet and nice but I have a weird side," says Valerie Galloway. "You can see it in my photos. The best ones have a film-still quality—something awkward and amateurish, like a strange Bulgarian porn film."

Galloway's work is sometimes dark, sometimes tender, and often somewhere in between. She started shooting when she was nineteen, "because I have a bad memory and I was afraid I'd forget I had even lived." It wasn't long before she began inviting friends to model for her, usually nude, before the simple black scrim that has served as a backdrop to all her portraits since. "There's usually vodka involved in my shoots," she says with a laugh. "It makes for better pictures."

But one guesses that Galloway herself is responsible for the ease with which her models pose together. She is the rare photographer—male or female—who prefers to photograph men. "People only think the female body is more beautiful because they see it more," says Galloway. "But look at Michelangelo's *David*, Al Pacino, young Marlon Brando." Gods indeed, but not at all like the men in these photos. Galloway's men are modern-day muses—lithe, pale, and dreamy eyed.

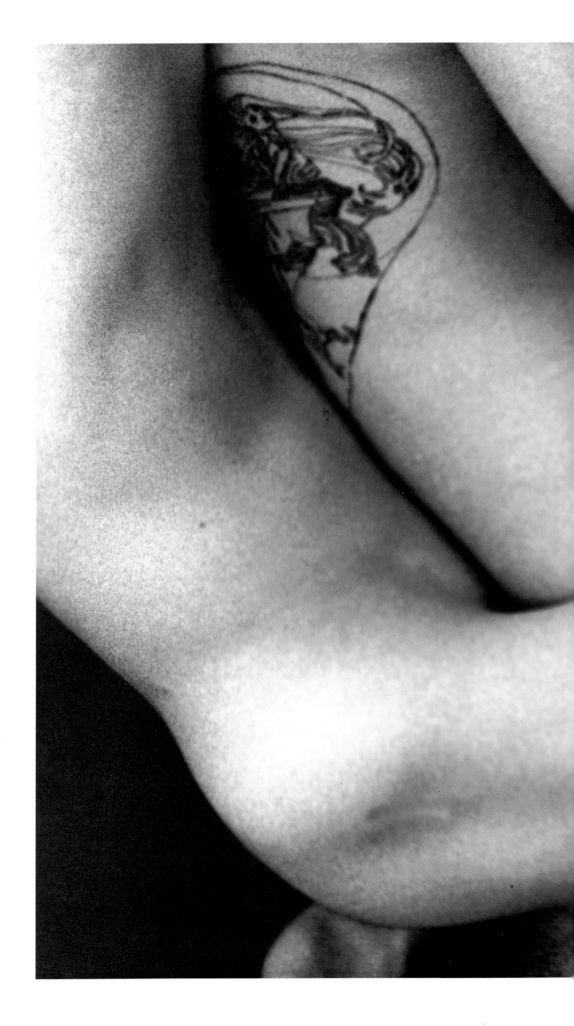

ROBERT ZVERINA /

Robert Zverina met his muse, Sasha, on a September afternoon in Prague: "We met at a little one-room English-language bookstore near Old Town Square where Sasha had been working part-time. We were immediately attracted to each other. She was so distracted she counted my change all wrong. I left my mailing address with her, because I didn't have a phone. Two days later there was a postcard inviting me out. After many beers and games of pool we went home together. We were insepa-rable for the remainder of our year in Prague."

The images shown here are two of the hundreds that Zverina shot of Sasha over the course of the next four years, as they followed each other back to the United States, to hotel rooms and apartments in Tampa, Manhattan, Brooklyn, Annapolis, and Baltimore. Although Robert always held the camera, theirs was an equal collaboration, producing a body of work as tender, sexy, and spontaneous as the rela-tionship it documents. "It was a long-distance thing so we'd go several months apart during which tension would mount, then there would

be a happy reunion over beer or red wine and several rolls of film," Zverina says. "We'd spend a couple of days inside, snapping and fucking, and then she'd be gone."

BARBARA VAUGHN /

Traveling from Death Valley's austere sand dunes to the driftwood-strewn coastline of the Pacific Northwest to the windy Sierra Nevada mountaintops, Barbara Vaughn has bared herself to the elements over the course of two years for this series of self-portraits. She has fallen off rocks, scraped herself raw on tree bark, and suffered head-to-toe insect bites, but these are minor inconveniences for Vaughn, who strives to emulate classical Greek sculpture against the Romantic back-drop of the great outdoors. Vaughn works alone, equipped with little more than her cam-era, a radio device that triggers her shutter while she poses, and a lucky denim shirt that's always at the ready on the not-so-unlikely occasion that she's discovered, naked, by a passerby. "In almost every setting, I am stumbled upon. Sometimes I'm warned by the sound of a car, footsteps, or breaking twigs, but I've been caught off guard. Most people are unnerved and turn away, but others are curious. Once, in Bermuda, I was in a secluded cove and a buck-naked man appeared over the rocks, insisting that I photograph him. That was one of the times it would have been nice to have an assistant." But Vaughn prefers to work solo, choreographing herself amid the natural shapes of each setting. She intends that the primary tension in the photograph be between body and landscape, so she rarely shows her face. "It reveals too much," she says. Her greatest challenge is to avoid the "deliberate sexuality" that the viewer expects to find in images of the nude form.

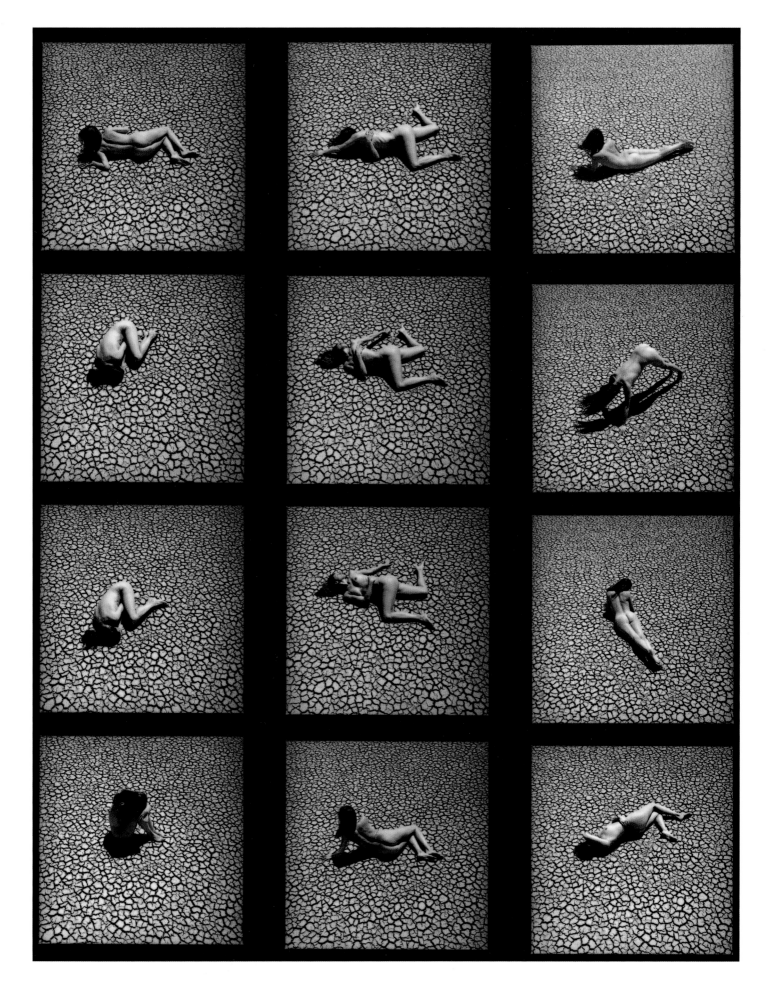

HOLGER MAASS /

German photographer Holger Maass prefers to leave the clinical minutia of naked bodies to the medical textbook publishers and pornographers. He's more interested in the fluid lines and curves, the warm shadows that give nudes their erotic character. "Because emotion, beauty, and eroticism take shape in our brains," says Maass, "it's much better to abandon the details, concentrate on the body as a whole, and let our minds fill in the blanks." By giving a preternatural, lambent glow to his subjects' skin, he imposes a sort of squinty vision on viewers, making it difficult for them to determine whether Maass' orange and green images are in fact blurred or their eyes are failing. As viewers take their cues from the few details that do manage to make their way through to the prints' surface in the form of fingerprints, nails, freckles, and hair, Maass hopes their imaginations will get a bit of exercise.

ANDREW EINHORN /

Andrew Einhorn calls himself "the king of comfort," and he's no mattress salesman. Einhorn prides himself on the fact that his models always enjoy the shoots as much as he does, and that "99 percent of them" like the results. This has much to do with the way he selects his models. (It also has to do with the models themselves: they tend to be lovely.) Einhorn is constantly walking or rollerblading the streets of New York in search of collaborators, who are mostly passersby or waitresses he meets on his coffee breaks. "I've always liked wait-

resses: they're cool looking." (Einhorn promises he'll shoot men soon; he just has to get comfortable with the idea.) He's been taking photos for seven years and says that once, maybe twice, his instincts were wrong. Einhorn can spot a good model by the way she walks, the way she holds herself. He knows how she'll move when she's naked because she talks with her hands, throws her head back when she laughs, looks over her shoulder and then out the window when she answers a question. And she doesn't run away when a

stranger invites himself home to shoot her naked.

SARAH A. FRIEDMAN /

Three years ago, the Internet was a foreign country to Sarah A. Friedman, whose techno-literacy started and stopped with her camera. That changed when her brother gave her his old laptop computer; within a week, Friedman had visited a host of Internet chatrooms, taking advantage of the opportunity to do one of her favorite things: start conversations with strangers. A woman with a strong sexual curiosity—she says she's never been afraid of anyone but herself—Friedman soon got the idea to post an ad for models in an Internet

classified section. Expose Yourself, it began. Fielding the scores of e-mail responses, primarily from men, Friedman chose most of the ones that didn't ask if she'd be getting nude too.

Friedman continues to work on the project in between shooting hip-hop artists for magazines like *Vibe* and *Blaze*. "My objective is to experience whoever responds to my ad," she says. "I enjoy exploring others' views of themselves via e-mail and then trying to translate those ideas visually. I'm learning more about

myself and my judgment and my boundaries; I'm learning to become more accepting, to find a part of myself in people that I believe I have little in common with."

JOHN F. COOPER /

John F. Cooper is afflicted with the familiar condition of "loving women," which is why he'd rather shoot female nudes than male. He admits such a preference could be a simple matter of sexual orientation, but artistically he finds the female form more graphic, more compelling. "With men, I'm disconnected, which can be a good thing, since there's no distraction; the process is all about form and the end result." But with female subjects, especially those with whom he's been romantically involved, the sexual tension adds a level of intensity and meaning to the process that is manifest in the final images.

Over the years, Cooper's artistic objective to make "fundamentally beautiful work" through the soft manipulation of light and texture has remained constant. He's worked toward his goal by taking the "quiet approach" to photography: "I'm deliberate in my work," he says. "I know what I'm going for, and I do it methodically, with respect." He also does it in black and white. "It's hard to shoot color in a conventional way," Cooper explains. "There's something inherently titillating about color, perhaps because it's more real. But my work is not about sex, it's about sensuality, and the black and white helps convey that because it's simply more abstract."

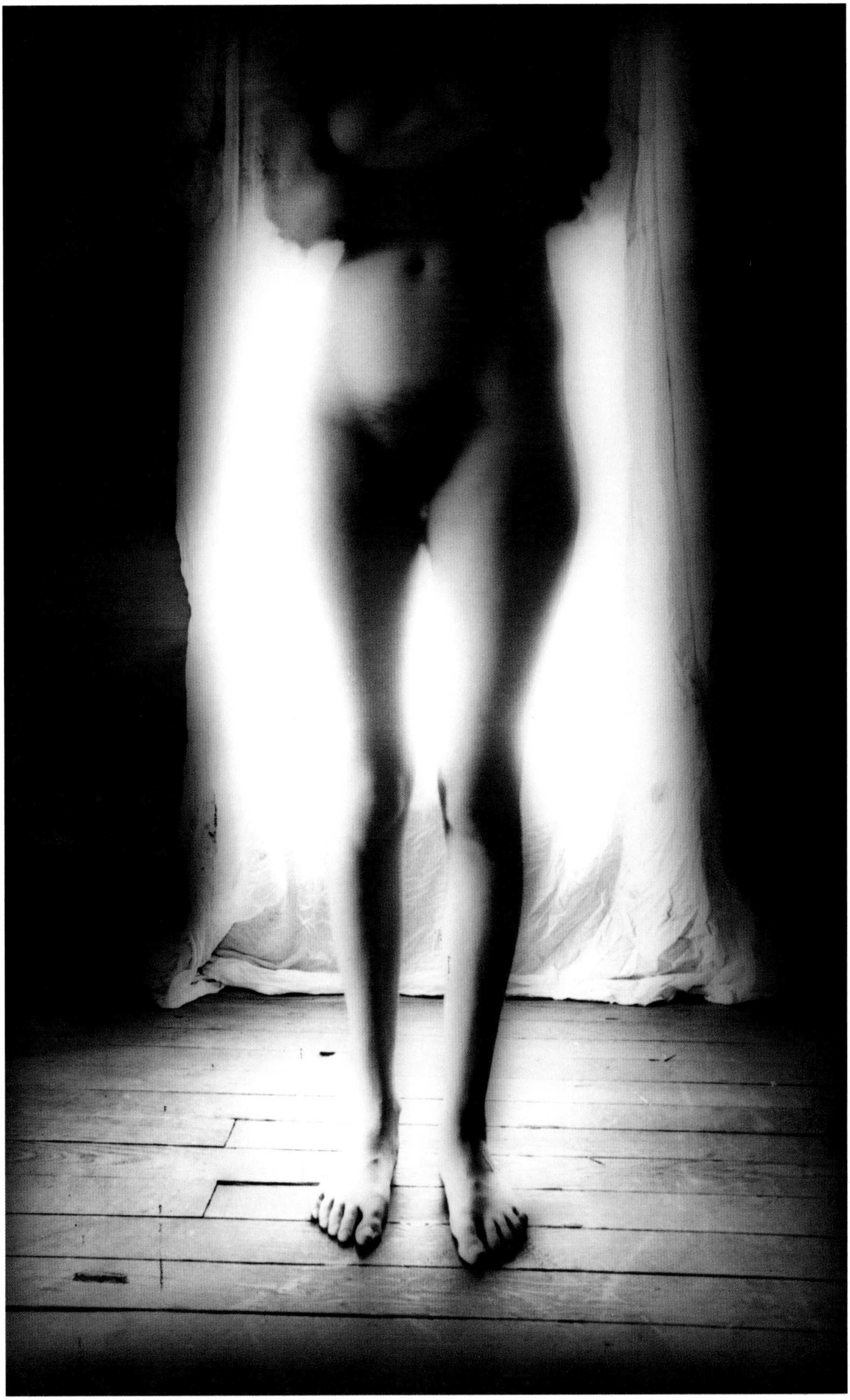

VALERIE PHILLIPS /

The first time Valerie Phillips visited the rambling Bronx, New York, house where these pictures were taken, she knew she had to return with her camera. She felt the same sense of instant recognition one night while having a drink with the woman who would eventually pose for Phillips in the old house. "I was mesmerized by her," says Phillips. "I'd been planning to street cast the shoot, but there was something about her that made me come right out and ask her to do it. She's enigmatic, interesting, and powerful—perfect for what I

wanted to do, because there wouldn't be any clothes to steal the scene. I ended up loving the pictures, which are sensuous, but not about sex at all. They're about her intelligence and personality and how she moves through her environment."

Phillips is often asked to explain why she shoots female nudes: "I'm not a feminist, nor am I against feminism," she says. "I don't feel it's my responsibility to address that. Most of the men I know are more obsessed with that issue than I am." Her preference for the female

body is explained with as much pragmatism: "Women are not who I'm sleeping with or necessarily sexually attracted to, so I can look at them without any preconceived framework. Besides that, I find women more mysterious and beautiful and intriguing."

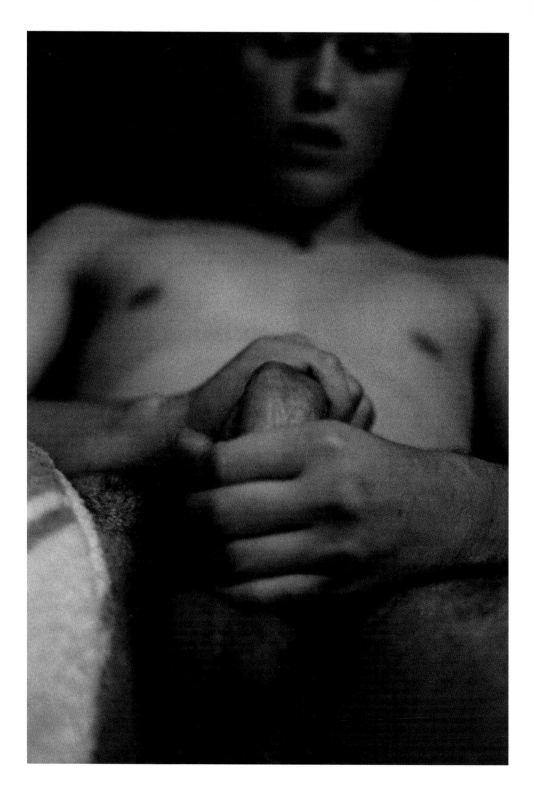

JANINE GORDON /

"I was never one of the girly girls," says Janine Gordon, who has spent the last decade photographing rockers and gang members, cops and hip-hoppers. It's tricky, she says, to be one of the guys and also be a girl who's more than mildly guy crazy. "Men think they can 'get over' when I'm taking pictures of them. I always have to keep myself one step ahead. Back in those days I didn't have any boundaries, but now I'm not as interested in being wild." She is interested in seeing what's behind the tough acts of the boys in her Brooklyn neighborhood. "These

guys were beautiful, and they were coming off stupid and tough. Macho is sexy, up to a point, but there has to be something underneath it."

In pointing her lens at both policemen and street kids, Gordon reveals a more political agenda: "I thought a lot of these kids were unrepresented and abused by the system. And I see how cops are. Mr. Tough Guys. When you take it all down, they have similar backgrounds. One cop said to me, 'Cops and robbers are just the same, we just wear different badges.'"

Gordon concentrates on the male figure, because "women have been painted and shot so much throughout history. I have to ask myself, Why should I keep this going forever? Why should I buy into this system?" Clearly, Gordon's take on feminism is more visceral than academic: "I like being tough," she says. "That's feminism to me."

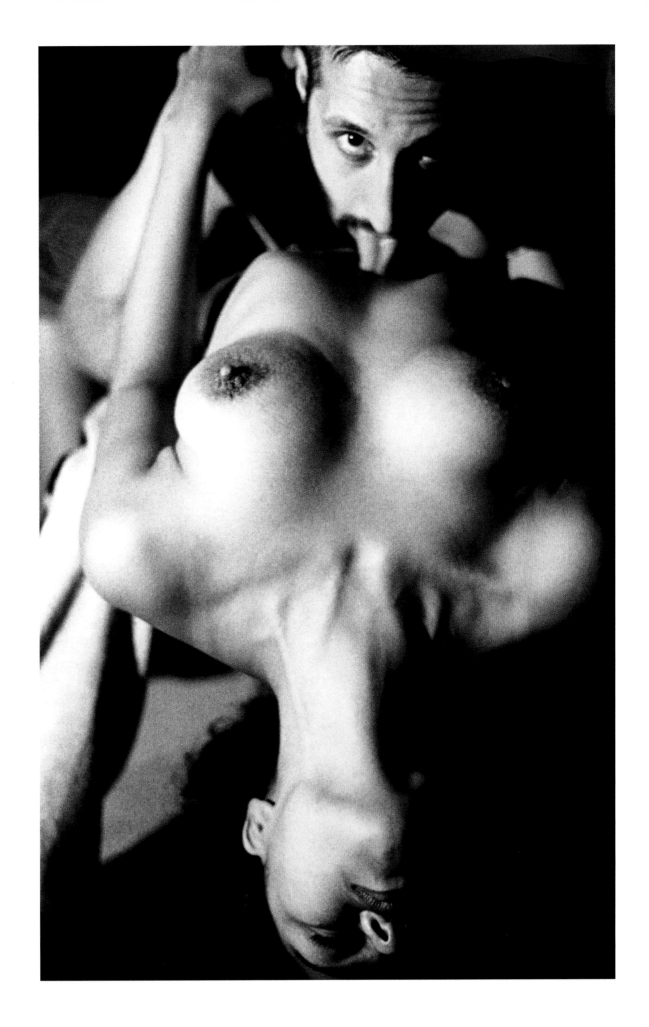

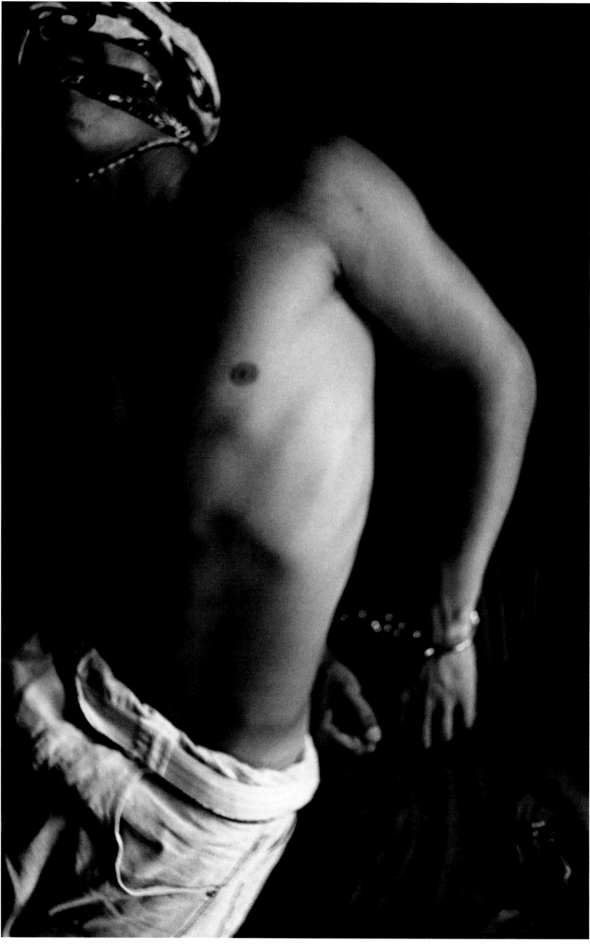

MARK BEARD /

Mark Beard's eye relishes all things timeless: a chef's uniform, an elegant pair of high heels, a nude figure. He believes that photography is "the retarded sibling of the arts" and considers it his mission to invest that branch with brains and dimension. "Hand anyone a camera to take three thousand photos and then give someone with taste a chance to pull their favorite sixty, and you'll have a beautiful collection," he declares. Though he doesn't see much merit in "accidental" beauty, Beard's own creative process involves plenty of trial and error;

the majority of his work ends up in the trash. The images in this series started as black-and-white photographs, which Beard painted over, then photographed with a Polaroid camera. Each Polaroid was then placed face down on wet etching paper. The end result is, in his words, "immediate and intimate at the same time," a hybrid of painting, printmaking, and photography. He has imbued these portraits with a hint of the surreal, yet they are thoughtful and restrained: "Not just a chance of light."

PETER J. GORMAN /

"One is never satisfied with a portrait of a person whom one knows," Goethe wrote. Peter Gorman saved himself the trouble; he only knew the subjects of these photographs for as long as he was behind the camera.

Gorman's living, as well as his art, is made through strangers. To pay the bills he shoots family portraits and actors' head shots. Both require attention to a subject's wishes: "I need to be aware of the things they like about themselves, the way they see themselves." Not so with this series. "These portraits are for me," he explained. "They're about how I see them and not who they actually are."

While shooting these portraits, Gorman found himself concerned mostly with stillness and the tiny gestures that emerge from boredom. "I would cross the room to change the film in the camera, and a model would start fiddling with the cross around her neck, and that would be the portrait. I'd tell her to freeze, and then I'd start shooting."

Gorman doesn't direct his characters according to a pre-existing script; instead he refines their movements and expressions. He makes them his own in the editing process—in the photograph he chooses and the fifty-nine he discards.

CHUCK SAMUELS /

In a famous photo by Helmut Newton, a raven-haired model stands regally in an opulent boarding room. She appears to be recovering, elegantly, from a car accident; one long leg is thigh high in a plaster cast, her neck is in a brace.

In a little-known photograph by the Canadian photographer Chuck Samuels, a man stands in an identical position, in an almost identical room, looking down his aquiline nose at the viewer. The image, *After Newton,* was (not incidentally) photo-graphed with the help of a female collaborator; it's one of twelve reconstructions of classic female nudes created by Samuels in his series "Before the Camera." Each of the collection parodies a staple image in the nude canon, from Man Ray's *Le Violon D'Ingres* to Richard Avedon's *Nastassja Kinski with Python* to Wynn Bullock's haunting *Child in the Forest* (shown here).

Samuels is an artist's artist. He is also a comedian with enough moxie to insert none other than himself—girlishly lithe, expertly made-up, and balding—as a geeky simulacrum of Nastassja Kinski and the "ailing" Jenny Capitain. It's this playful side of Samuels that will charm even those whose knowledge of photography begins and ends with Helmut Newton.

Most of us take for granted that, like the photographers parodied in Samuels' travesty, we're more comfortable ogling the female body than the male. It's a rarity when a man steps in front of the camera to remind us of just how absurd that is.

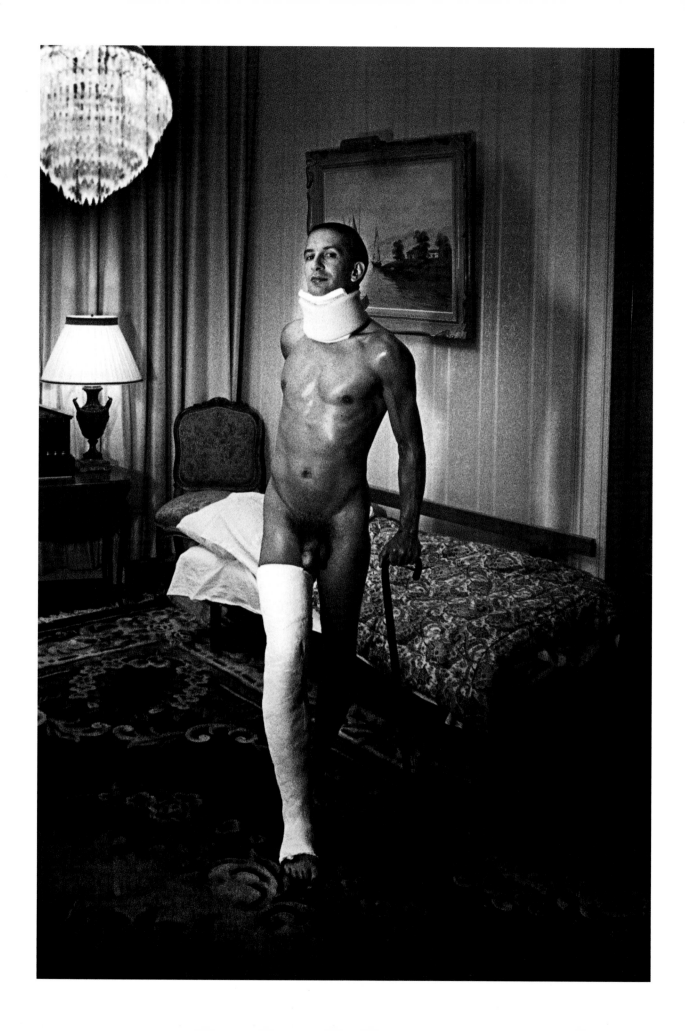

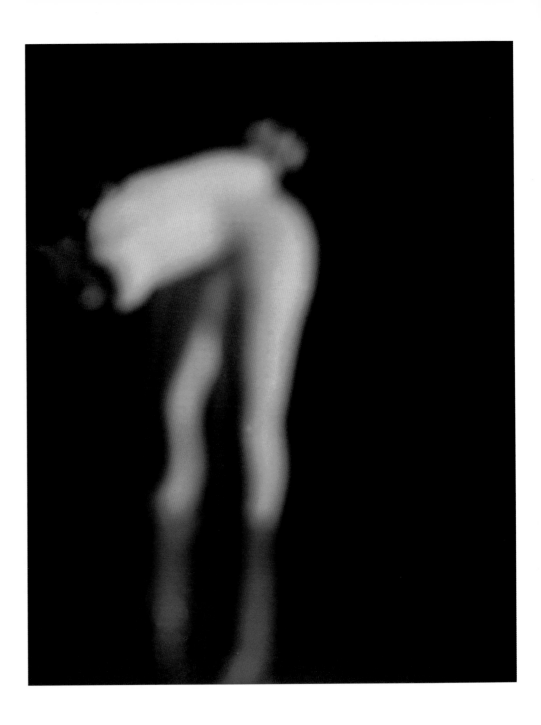

DAVID LEVINTHAL /

David Levinthal created his "Desire" series with a Polaroid camera and several six-inch Barbie-like Japanese figurines of Caucasian women in bondage. The nature of female sexuality lies at the center of Levinthal's photographs, which examine the way desire, and its image, are manufactured. The photographs are blurred until the palm-sized figurines (whose dismembered, polyurethane limbs are sold by catalogue) translate into surprisingly gentle and animate representations of desire. At Levinthal's first gallery show, he was asked to clarify which pictures were of live humans and which of plastic toys. It turns out that they were all plastic; but in a world in which most images of women are enhanced by silicone or silicon technology, Levinthal's work self-consciously mocks our difficulty distinguishing between organic and inorganic, actual and virtual.

"I think my intention was to explore the idea of voyeuristic sexuality," says Levinthal. "To me these photographs should be upsetting. They are beautiful. I wanted to draw viewers in and then have them say, 'Wait a minute, I'm looking at this beautiful image but it's also horrible.' Some people will relate to this work purely as erotic, and other people will be very upset by it. I wanted viewers to be self-reflective, to think about what it is that draws them to this work."

KATRINA DEL MAR /

Del Mar means "of the sea," but Katrina del Mar is all concrete. She says "fucking" all the time in her New Jersey accent; she lives in leather jeans and combat boots; she stays up all night and works all day. Against stark backgrounds, del Mar shoots ex-junkies (current junkies tend not to show up), the physically altered (via surgery, tattoos, or severe diets), and others who live to flip off convention. Her subjects seem unashamed, and often angry. Theirs is that hard glamor peculiar to New York, the most "city" of all cities.

What separates del Mar's work from that of the better-known, but equally hard-edged, underground–New York photographer, Richard Kern?

"Half a generation and my pussy."

Another difference is that del Mar will on occasion perfectly contradict her own style, revealing an ultraexposed, tender side: her photos can be all bare feet, cautious embraces, and a lot of pregnant bellies. "I shoot men who are more overtly vulnerable, smiling. Men tend to look like teenage girls

in my pictures."

And the women tend to look like . . . ?

"Teenage girls. Ha! Teenage girls in gangs."

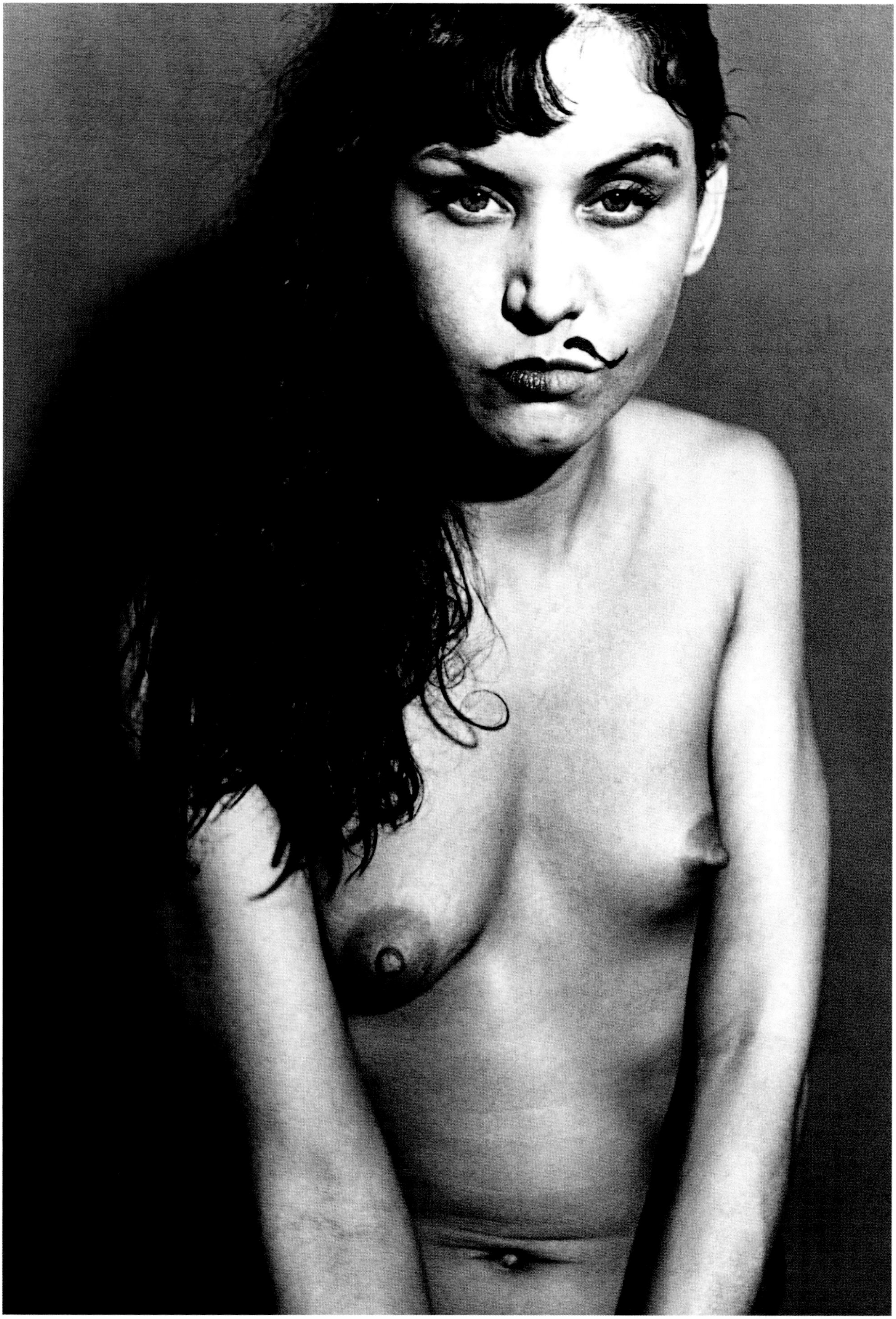

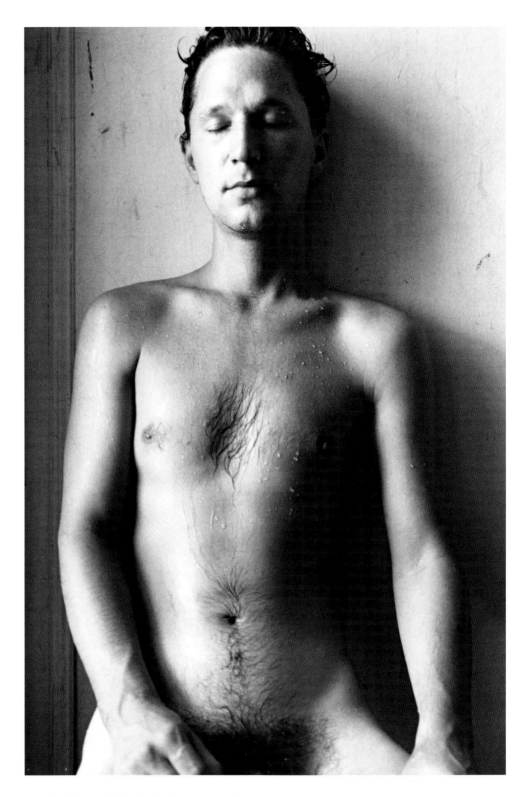

VIVIENNE MARICEVIC /

When Vivienne Maricevic was a little girl, her mother took her to Times Square and the traveling circus, where they would people watch for hours. Her fascination with difference did not end with childhood. Maricevic has spent the last twenty years photographing people on the sexual fringes of society—drag queens, transvestites, transsexuals, porn stars, and fetishists—as well as more typical men with their clothes off.

There has certainly been no pictorial shortage of naked women throughout photo-graphic history. But just try to find some male nudes that aren't perfect hairless Greek gods—it's not easy. So twenty years ago, hoping to fill that void, Maricevic undressed her then-boyfriend, took out her camera, and started shooting. She hasn't stopped since.

For Maricevic, these photographs cele-brate the beauty of character and personality expressed through gesture and poise rather than the fantasy of "perfect outer shells."

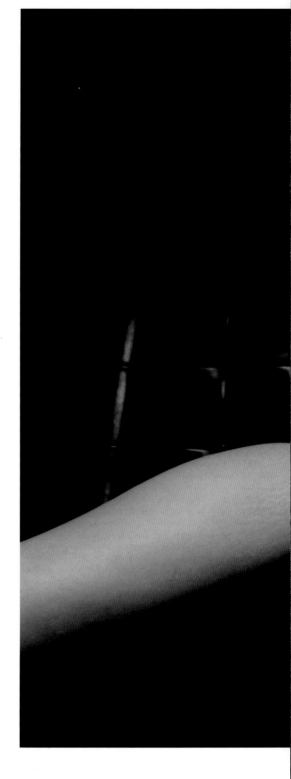

RICHARD LOHR /

Richard Lohr, a fashion photographer in London for eighteen years, moved to New York City six years ago when the Brits' hipster coolness started leaving him cold.

Had he not become an ex-pat, Lohr probably wouldn't have started doing nude work. He explains: "The English are very dirty minded in a nudge-nudge, wink-wink sort of way. They're big on sexual innuendo and can turn everything into a dirty joke. Nude photography is often all tits and ass to them and not much more. But in New York, a city with such a cul-tural appetite for photography, people are much more willing to look at a picture of a nude woman and see something more meaningful."

Lohr says he subscribes to the view that everyone has an aesthetic allure that can be captured by a sensitive photographer. And, for him, getting at it is a lot easier when his subjects are naked. "There's no lying at that point, no other consideration. And they get a buzz from the realization that someone else can find them so worthy of attention in such a basic state." That buzz animates his photos and belies the darkness of their composition. Their absence of light speaks not of something sad or sinister, but of warmth and richness, comfort and confidence.

GEORGE PITTS /

George Pitts is a painter, photographer, writer, and would-be filmmaker. A Pitts film, one guesses, would feature plenty of long-legged, melancholic women with bad posture and bad habits. His heroines would apply their makeup in poorly lit mirrors and sleep too much, but they'd always be smarter than the men they loved and hated. But maybe Pitts will be content to pay homage to his favorite art house filmmakers—Jean-Luc Godard, Rainer Werner Fassbinder, George Cukor—in photographs like these. In them are traces of what Pitts calls Godard's "passionate yet detached way of looking at women," but the women who pose for Pitts are more reminiscent, in their steely-eyed vulnerability, of the seamy goddesses in Fassbinder's *The Marriage of Maria Braun*.

Pitts loves the way Fassbinder "dumped the most beautiful aspects of his persona onto his heroines," but he himself gravitates toward models whose stories, one thinks, would fill volumes. And like the best kind of narrators, they leave us wanting to know more.

WOLFGANG TILLMANS /

Eager to classify the work of Wolfgang Tillmans, early observers picked up on the prevalence of youth in his seemingly spontaneous photographs, labeling the photographer a documentarian of his generation. The truth was more complex, and not just because of the extent to which Tillmans was collaborating with his models to "impersonate" the idea of themselves that they and Tillmans were interested in seeing. ("I don't photograph them as friends," he once said. "They are impersonators of their own and my ideas.") In fact, Tillmans was adjusting the sober code of the documentary in order to convey a measure of emotional engagement with his youthful subjects, whose self-presentation was often awkward and exhibitionistic. Tillmans resents the wholesale dismissal of this aspect of youth as only a "phase." And while it is above all his individual pictures of young people that illustrate the extent to which the self is always a work in progress, his signature (re-)arrangements of those pictures in magazine spreads, books, and installations have provided him with a means of coming to grips with his own mutable state of selfhood as a gay man.

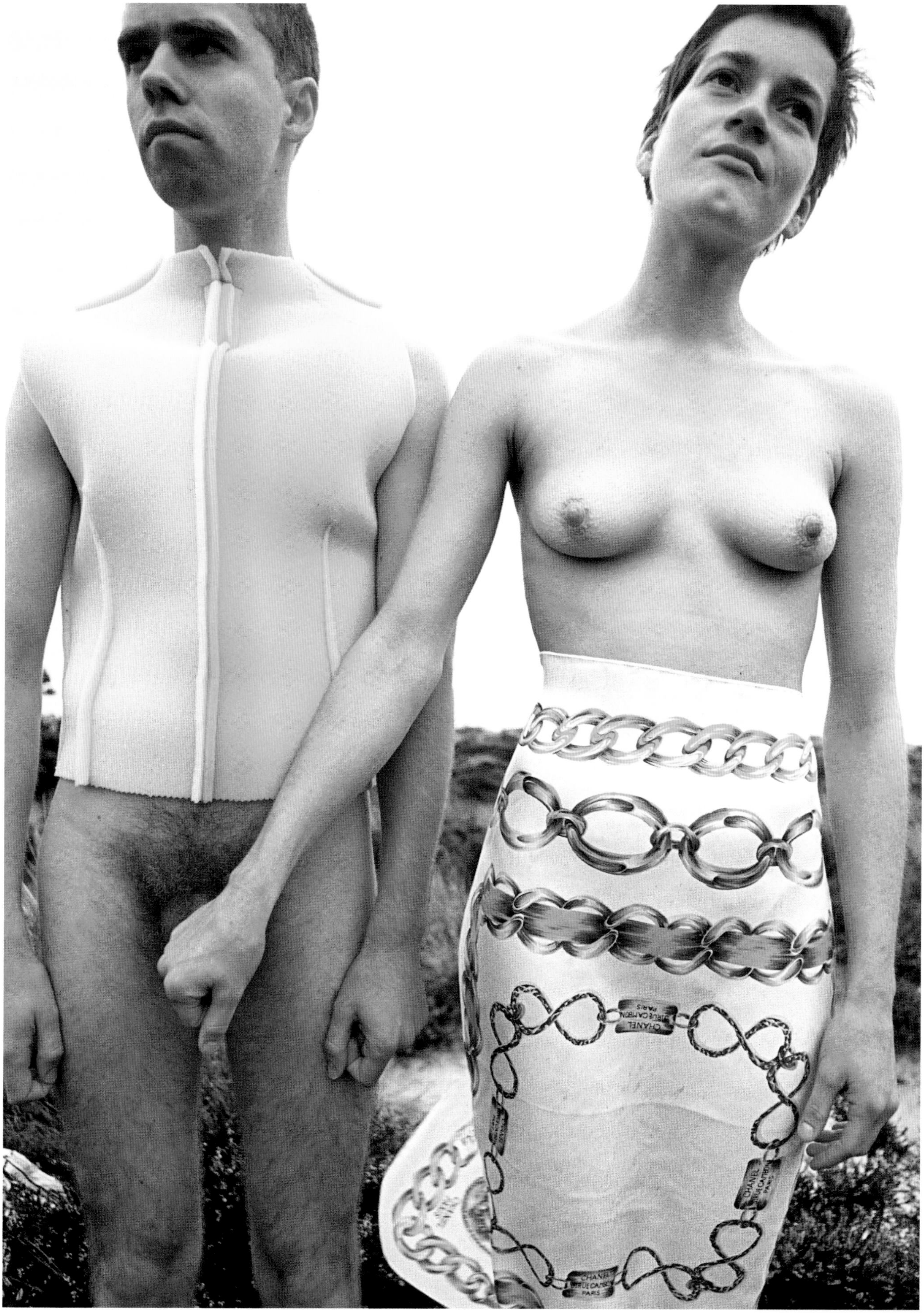
CHANEL
31 RUE CAMBON
PARIS

SAKIKO NOMURA /

In Sakiko Nomura's native Japan, where art and sexuality, at least to a Westerner's eye, seem inextricable, a new school of artists is challenging their nation's sexual traditions and taboos. The most visible of these provocateurs, Noboyushi Araki, has become a celebrity of American-rock-star proportions.

Young enough to be Araki's daughter (and, incidentally, employed by him as an assistant), Sakiko Nomura is lesser known but, in spite of herself, seems to have as strong a knack for causing a stir. Several pictures from this series were seized en route to an exhibition in Austria by Japanese authorities. (In Japan, any depiction of pubic hair is censored; Nomura doesn't comment, but this may explain her models' shadowed genitals in these prints.)

But unlike Araki's harder-edged pictures of women, Nomura's black-and-white snapshots of her male friends lounging naked in crisp hotel rooms are more poignant than pornographic—it's the *fact* of them that's subversive. Although women, and libidinous ones at that, are endlessly depicted in Japanese art—from traditional *ukiyo-e* wood-block prints to modern anime—rarely does the female artist create erotic art involving men.

Nomura's authorship of these pictures isn't the only contradiction they present. Her men are seductively feminine, their postures devoid of machismo; they surrender to her lens like patient lovers, yet their relationship to Nomura is unclear. Perhaps this ambiguity is intentional—Nomura's way of saying that she is as sexually complex as her subjects.

ELINOR CARUCCI /

From one's first fleeting glance there is an aching familiarity about Elinor Carucci's photographs. Carucci is a young Israeli ex-pat, now living with her husband in New York's West Village. Her varied oeuvre is made up exclusively of moments captured from her own life—all interior shots, all featuring herself and/or members of her family in various states of disrobe— as abstracted details or as full, dramatic tableaus. Shadows fall heavily and redraw frames within the frame.

Though Carucci describes her work in terms of archetypes—intimacy, family, love, career—such universalism could easily be undermined by the specificity of her world: a glamorously beautiful and liberal family; the cultures of Jerusalem and New York that share the background space; subjects who have been "trained" for more than fifteen years to ignore the presence of the tripod, the strobe, the tungsten lights. Yet Carucci's photographs demonstrate that gestures, light, mood, and shapes can tran-

scend the particularity of a situation and speak more broadly to "life experience." Pointing to a picture titled *Eran and I, 1998* (see Introduction), in which Carucci lies bare breasted and serene across the foreground, her husband's face tucked into her neck, one of his eyes just visible above her collarbone, she explains, "This is about love. See the way he fits perfectly into my shape?"

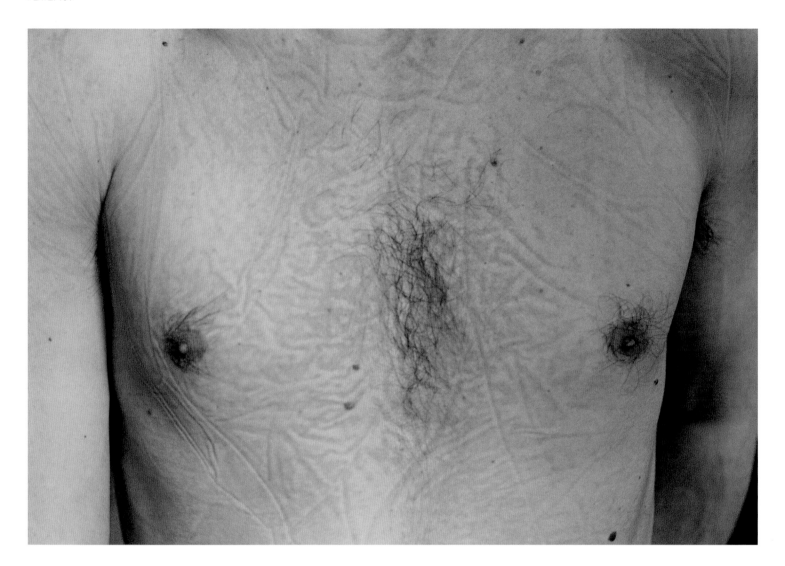

LYLE ASHTON HARRIS /

Lyle Ashton Harris says his work is not "about fitting into any one category concerning race, gender, or sexuality; it's about the space that exists in between." In this space, Harris finds "pleasure, ambivalence, beauty, ambiguity."

As a person, Harris is as surprising as his portraits are mysterious. Before his whiteface phase, illustrated here by *Miss America,* he was an economics major at Wesleyan University, taking intimate, diaristic portraits of his friends. "They were about desire. About beauty. About what happened before and after the caught moment as much as what you see." It was more than a decade after he took a picture of a dear friend, Michelle, lying amid an array of historical drawings that Harris decided to print the image. Rediscovering *Michelle,* along with other images from over the years, has given Harris a new body of work through which to address his favorite themes: "These pictures speak of a certain absence by their articulation of desire," he says. "I'm interested in how images function as documents of loss."

ONDREA BARBE /

Ondrea Barbe often shoots people who are beautiful in places that are not: amid the rubble of a vacant lot, peeking through a chain-link fence, or here, in the crumbling kitchen she shares with her boyfriend, Michael. In this case, the models are Ondrea and Michael themselves, who couldn't care less if their bath-tub serves double duty as a dishwasher.

    This picture is Barbe's attempt to capture not only the affinity between Michael and her but also "the universal want between two people in love." She has distilled a refreshing sense of abandon, one that rarely happens for photographers who usually must settle for playing third wheel as a couple interacts. (Ondrea has also put herself to that test, with a series about "two women exploring bisexuality as an extension of their own femininity.") And no doubt she will continue to document her relationship with Michael, who is happy to oblige: "I spent most of my life alone, drifting, and now I'm set," he says of Ondrea. "There's no need to explore any fur-ther. I've found the one I want."

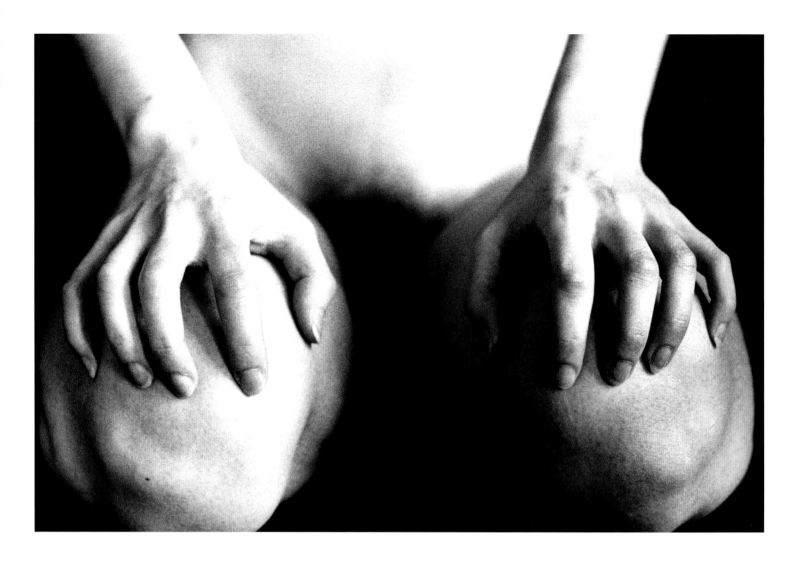

RALPH GIBSON /

Most photography lovers have a Ralph Gibson image catalogued somewhere in their memory. Chances are at least one of the young artists included in this book taped a postcard reproduction of some ethereal Gibson tableau to her wall, years before her own work would take its place. Still, Gibson may have more in common, aesthetically and philosophically, with his mentors, the portraitists Dorothea Lange and Bill Brandt, than with the up-and-coming generation of photographers who have followed in his footsteps. Next to the postmodern work of an artist like Wolfgang Tillmans, Gibson's nudes are studies in formalism. Classically influenced ("It is almost as if the light is the subject, and the woman is the source of light"), Gibson may also be the first master photographer to subvert "fine art" by concerning himself equally with the female body's geometry and its sexuality; his photographs are as much about his passion for women as his passion for light.

ANDRES SERRANO /

Look closely at these images: it will be hard to forget them. Now imagine yourself surrounded by all twenty of the larger-than-life cibachromes that comprise Serrano's series "A History of Sex." The mental exercise alone may leave you unsettled.

The seasoned art lovers at the unveiling of Serrano's "History" series were a jaded lot. They had stomached his previous two exhibits—"The Morgue," a horrifyingly beautiful festival of dead bodies in saturated color, and before that, "Fluids," featuring *Piss Christ,*

the urine-drenched crucifix that was ripped up by Alphonse D'Amato on the Senate floor and sledgehammered by a zealous visitor to the National Gallery of Victoria, in Melbourne, Australia. But no amount of savvy could have prepared Serrano's patrons for *Red Pebbles,* in which a crouching woman tentatively holds a horse's penis, or *Fisting,* a gentle, X-rated portrait of a hairless, naked man and an unsmiling woman wearing a long dress and a large silver cross.

"A History of Sex" (which was completed

in the Netherlands at the invitation of the Groninger Museum) is a shock for some; others find the scenes as natural as the ocean and open fields that serve as its backdrops. Serrano, who is fascinated with "how sexual imagery and practice should be dealt with publicly," is no doubt pleased with both responses.

Ondrea Barbe has had her photographs published in *Time Out NY, Photo District News,* and *Picture.* She has worked commercially for Polygram in France and New York, as well as for Elite, Ford, Hourra, and Marilyn Gauthier modeling agencies. She is currently working on a magazine called *Moxy.*

Mark Beard's work appears in the collections of the Whitney Museum of American Art, the Metropolitan Museum of Art, the Toledo Museum of Fine Art, the Utah Museum of Art, Yale University, Harvard University, the New York Public Library, and the Graphische Sammlung in Munich. He continues to discover paintings created by his late alter ego, Bruce Sargeant (1848–1938), who worked in the 1920s and 1930s.

Alvin Booth was born in Hull, an industrial city in the northeast of England. His work has been shown in numerous one-person and group exhibitions. His first book is entitled *Corpus: Beyond the Body.*

Thomas Carabasi's fine art photography has been exhibited both nationally and internationally, including shows in Australia, Germany, and Italy. Sarasota's Ringling Museum, Tucson's Center for Creative Photography, the Philadelphia Museum of Art, and the Museo Ken Damy in Italy all carry his work in their collections; *Popular Photography, ZOOM* magazine, *Mirabella, Interiors,* the *New York Times,* and the *London Independent* newspaper have all published his photography.

An Israeli ex-pat, **Elinor Carucci** received her B.A. in photography at Bezalel Academy of Arts and Design, Jerusalem. Her work is collected at the Houston Museum of Fine Arts, the Brooklyn Museum of Arts, and the Museum of Israeli Art.

John F. Cooper is a Manhattan-based photographer whose work has appeared in *Allure, Elle, GQ, Mademoiselle, Seventeen,* and *Vogue* as well as in the anthologies *Nude York* and *Sensual Images.* His experiments with Polaroid transfers have also gained him a place in the Polaroid Permanent Collection.

Renee Cox's photography has been seen in many exhibitions of art about gender and race, including the Whitney Museum's "Black Male," the Aldrich Museum's "No Doubt: African-American Artists in the '90s," and the New Museum of Contemporary Art's "Picturing the Modern Amazon." She was selected for the 1999 Venice Bienale and has received grants for photography from the Ford Foundation, among many other foundations.

Jessica Craig-Martin has been a regular contributor to *Vogue* since 1997. After holding editorial positions at *British Vogue,* the *Sunday Telegraph,* and *Vanity Fair,* she switched entirely to a career as a photographer. Her work has been shown at the Pat Hearn Gallery, White Columns, the Boesky Kallery Gallery, and the New Museum of Contemporary Art. She also contributes regularly to the *New York Times Magazine, Elle Décor,* and *Art & Auction* and is a contributing editor at *Index.*

Katrina del Mar photographs people: tattooed women, rock stars, transgendered punk rockers shaving in the bathtub, and so forth. She publishes *Plushtoy Catalog.*

Andrew Einhorn has been photographing nudes since the early 1990s. A journalism graduate from Temple University, he has always had a passion for the people side of photography and thrives on the challenge of convincing others that posing is good for their health. He plans to put out a book as soon as he can get famous from his cable access TV show, *Dog the Cat.*

FiLH (Frédéric Goudal) has been in a serious committed relationship with photography for five years (they had just been dating for seven years before that). He's done the traditional framed-work-on-a-wall exhibitions in Bordeaux, but his main showcase is the Internet, where he can more easily let it all hang out.

Greg Friedler was born in 1970 and grew up in New Orleans, Louisiana. He received a M.F.A. in photography from the School of Visual Arts in New York City. He has published three books, *Naked New York, Naked Los Angeles,* and *Naked London.*

Sarah A. Friedman is an instructor at the School of Visual Arts in New York. Her photographs have been published in *Vibe, Spin, Blaze, Fortune,* and *Newsweek.* She has also shot for Reebok, Atlantic Records, and Tommy Boy Records.

Valerie Galloway lives in Brooklyn, New York. She works at a photography studio and takes pictures in her spare time.

Charles Gatewood's photography has been supported by three fellowships from the New York State Council on the Arts, awards from the American Institute of Graphic Arts, the Art Directors' Club and *Photographer's Forum,* as well as the Leica Medal of Excellence for Outstanding Humanistic Photojournalism. His books include *Charles Gatewood, Sidetripping* (with William S. Burroughs), *Wall Street, Primitives,* and *True Blood.*

Ralph Gibson's photographs are in the permanent collections of the Metropolitan Museum of Art, the Museum of Modern Art, the Whitney Museum of American Art, the National Gallery in Washington, D.C., and other museums and galleries throughout the world. He has been awarded a Guggenheim and three National Endowment for the Arts Fellowships. In his spare time, he plays the electric guitar.

Nan Goldin has exhibited her work in numerous solo and group exhibitions; among the most important was her mid-career retrospective at the Whitney Museum of American Art in 1996. She has published many books and catalogues, including *The Ballad of Sexual Dependency.* She is the recipient of a National Endowment for the Arts award.

Janine Gordon studied art and writing at Cooper Union and at New York University. Her work has been seen in various shows around the world. She had her first solo show at the John Gibson Gallery in 1995. She is working on two new series, "Hardcore Hip-Hop" and "Boy Stories." She has written reviews and articles for *Flash Art* and works occasionally for *XXL* and *Blaze* magazine as a freelance photographer.

Peter J. Gorman was born in 1961 in Binghamton, New York. His obsession with photographing nudes began when he bought his first camera at age sixteen and began shooting his girlfriend. Peter has worked since college as a photographer and contributes regularly to *Black Book* magazine. He lives in New York with his wife, Rachel.

Camella Grace is a Los Angeles–based adventure seeker, photographer, filmmaker, and computer geek.

Lyle Ashton Harris received his M.F.A. from the California Institute for the Arts and has also studied at the Tisch School of the Arts and the Whitney Museum's Independent Study Program in New York. Harris has exhibited at the Guggenheim Museum, the Kunsthalle in Basel, Switzerland, the Whitney Museum of American Art, and the Institute of Contemporary Art in London. His work is included in the permanent collections of the Museum of Fine Arts in Boston, the Museum of Contemporary Art in San Diego, and many private collections.

Thomas Karsten's work has appeared in many magazines and photo journals, including *Stern, Das Magazin, Art, Capital,* and *Eltern.* He published his first collection of photos entitled *Thomas— mach ein Bild von uns!* (Thomas, take our picture!) in 1988, followed by *Messer im Traum—Transsexuelle in Deutschland* (Knife in a Dream: Transsexuals in Germany) in 1994.

Richard Kern studied art and philosophy at the University of North Carolina at Chapel Hill. His films have been shown at the Whitney Museum of American Art. A second edition of his book, *New York Girls,* was published in June 1997. A new collection of his photographs is being published by Taschen.

Marcelo Krasilcic is a Brazilian photographer who has lived in New York City since 1990. His photographs have appeared in *Purple, Spin, Harper's Bazaar, Newsweek, The Face, Cosmopolitan, Artforum, Detour,* and *Vogue Homme International* as well as on album covers for artists such as Everything but the Girl and the Marvelous Three.

David Levinthal received his M.F.A. in photography from Yale University. He is the recipient of fellowships from the Guggenheim Foundation and the N.E.A. His book *Mein Kampf* received France's Prix du Livres de Photographies. He has published twelve books and catalogues; his latest is *Barbie Millicent Roberts (An Original),* published in the fall of 1998.

Canadian-born photographer **Richard Lohr** spent most of his adult life in London working primarily in fashion. Since an enlightening filmmaking expedition to Tibet (which put the fashion world into a new perspective for him), he has been able to take on more commissions in the field he calls "real photography." Lohr now lives in New York City.

Leslie Lyons' photography has appeared in *Vibe, Black and White, Time Out New York, Wavelength,* and in various group shows.

Holger Maass worked as a self-taught photographer while studying electrical engineering at college in Germany. Since then, he's shot several major German magazine features as well as ad campaigns for various agencies and companies. He won the silver Deutscher Direktmarketing Preis in 1996 and the Deutsch-Französischen Gesellschaft award in 1997. Maass runs his own studio in Munich.

Vivienne Maricevic has worked as a picture researcher for *True* magazine, an exhibits editor for *Camera Arts* magazine, and as the photo editor for Crescent Publishing Group. Her work has been exhibited at the International Center of Photography, the Houston Center for Photography, and Nikon House in New York. She is the recipient of a New York Foundation for the Arts Fellowship. Her recent book of photographs of transvestites and male-to-female transsexuals is entitled *Male to Female: La Cage aux Folles.*

Robert Maxwell is a former surfer who shoots for *W, Vogue, Vibe, Entertainment Weekly,* and *Vanity Fair.* He is at work on a book of his photographs.

Sean McDevitt has been featured in solo exhibitions at the Dru Arstark gallery in New York, 7 Stages in Atlanta, and the Lamar Dodd School of Art at the University of Georgia. He has also participated in numerous group exhibitions, including shows held at White Columns, Jim Kempner Fine Art, and the Loyola Gallery downtown in New Orleans, to name a few.

Ian McFarlane's photographs have appeared in the *Photo Review,* the *Georgia Review,* and *B&W.* He has been the still photographer on several music videos, most notably for R.E.M. and the Dave Matthews Band. He currently resides in Athens, Georgia.

Sakiko Nomura currently lives and works in Tokyo, Japan. Her work has been shown in solo exhibitions in Tokyo at the Egg Gallery, Apt Gallery, Gallery Verita, and Gallery Eve. Her photographs were recently published in the book *Japanese Photography: Desire and Void.* She has been the studio assistant to Nobuyoshi Araki since 1991.

Valerie Phillips lives between North London and Murray Hill, New York, and has most recently shot for *Sleaze Nation, Details, Esquire,* and *Nylon.* She is midway through an acclaimed and contentious two-year faux-documentary ad campaign for the Liverpool nightclub Cream. She is currently working on a book about Brooklyn teenagers.

George Pitts, the picture editor for *Vibe* magazine, is a published writer and artist whose work has been shown in numerous group exhibitions. *American Photo* has cited him as one of nineteen "movers and shakers for the future."

Sylvia Plachy is a staff photographer for the *Village Voice.* Her first book, *Unguided Tour,* won the International Center for Photography Infinity Award for Best Publication of 1990. Her work appears in the collections of the Musuem of Modern Art and the Metropolitan Museum of Art and the Bibliothèque Nationale in Paris. She has had solo exhibitions at the Whitney Museum of American Art and other venues. She is a recipient of the Guggenheim Fellowship Award.

Terry Richardson was born in New York City in the middle of the swinging sixties. After an epiphany in Tompkins Square Park in the early 1980s, he tossed aside his rock-and-roll dreams and began his photo documentation of the East Village underground scene. Since then, his fashion photographs and celebrity portraits have appeared in *W, Harper's Bazaar, British Vogue, Spin, The Face,* and *Allure,* among many other magazines.

Chuck Samuels' photography is collected in the Canadian Museum of Contemporary Photography and has been exhibited in galleries throughout Canada, the United States, and Europe.

Andres Serrano studied photography at the Brooklyn Museum Art School in New York. He has received grants from the New York State Council on the Arts, the National Endowment for the Arts, and other foundations. His photography has been exhibited at museums around the world, including the Whitney Museum of American Art, the Museum of Contemporary Art, and the National Museum of Photography. *Body and Soul* is a bound collection of his work.

Taryn Simon has studied photography at the Rhode Island School of Design and at Spéos Photographic Institute in Paris, France. She has been published in French *Vogue, L'uomo Vogue, Visionaire, i-D, Big,* and the *New York Times Magazine,* among other magazines. She has had work in exhibitions in Paris and New York.

Robert Stivers has shown his work extensively in the United States and Europe. His photographs are in the collections of the Los Angeles County Museum of Art, the Museum Ludwig, and the Victoria and Albert Museum of Art. He has published one book, *Robert Stivers: Photographs,* and is soon to publish a second.

Hiroshi Sunairi was born in Hiroshima in 1972. He came to the United States at the age of eighteen to study. At S.U.N.Y. Purchase, Hiroshi evolved from the study of painting to performance art, video art, installation art, and photography. He has exhibited at the Andrew Kreps Gallery.

Wolfgang Tillmans was born in Germany and studied at Bournemouth & Poole College of Art & Design in England. His photography first appeared in *i-D* and has since appeared in galleries, publications, and museums throughout the world. He is copublisher of the magazine *Spex.*

The photographs of **Arthur Tress** are included in the collections of the Museum of Modern Art, the Metropolitan Museum of Art, the Whitney Museum of American Art, the International Center of Photography, Centre Georges Pompidou, and others. He has published eleven books of photography, including the forthcoming *Male of the Species.*

Barbara Vaughn is a New York–based portrait photographer whose clothed clients include celebrities, corporate executives, rock bands, authors, artists, and families. Her nude clients include women in all the above-mentioned categories and more. A former competitive figure skater, she spent several years in the corporate world before pursuing her passion for photography as a career.

Tony Ward received his M.F.A. from the Rochester Institute of Technology before working as a staff photographer for a pharmaceutical house and eventually giving up corporate photography to pursue portraiture and photo-eroticism. His work has been exhibited around the world and published in *Life, Penthouse, American Photo,* and other magazines.

Phillip Wong's photography has periodically appeared in *Italian Vogue,* German *Playboy,* and American *Penthouse.*

Robert Zverina studied poetry with Allen Ginsberg, who taught him to always have a camera on hand. His *Picture of the Day* website is a tribute to life as seen out of the corner of one's eye.

PHOTO CAPTIONS

Ondrea Barbe
140 From the *Want* series

Mark Beard
104 *Aiden with Ugly Fruit*,
1998, Polaroid transfer
print, courtesy Wessel +
O'Connor Gallery
105 *"I am ten years older than
Aiden. He would call me
dad and then laugh. I
washed him, after fucking,
like a father,"* 1992,
Polaroid transfer print,
courtesy Wessel +
O'Connor Gallery
106 *Untitled (Male Torso)*,
Polaroid transfer print,
courtesy Wessel +
O'Connor Gallery
107 *"Aiden is vulnerable. He
makes pop videos, he
showed them our second
night. He read a long letter
from a friend to explain who
he was,"* 1992, Polaroid
transfer print, courtesy
Wessel + O'Connor Gallery

Alvin Booth
043 *Untitled*
044 *Untitled*

Thomas Carabasi
037 *Arabesque*, 1987
038 *Dian's Worshippers*, 1987

Elinor Carucci
001 *Eran and I*, 1998, courtesy
Ricco/Maresca Gallery
133 *Eran and I in Bathroom*,
1994, courtesy
Ricco/Maresca Gallery
134 *Eran's Chest in the
Morning*, 1999, courtesy
Ricco/Maresca Gallery
135 *Mirror Reflection*, 1998,
courtesy Ricco/Maresca
Gallery
136 *Eran and the Computer*,
1997, courtesy
Ricco/Maresca Gallery

John F. Cooper
095 *Untitled*
096 *Untitled*
097 *Untitled*

Renee Cox
053 *Yo Mama at Home*, courtesy Cristinerose Gallery
054 *Yo Mama*, courtesy
Cristinerose Gallery
055 *Hot-En-Tot*, courtesy
Cristinerose Gallery
056 *Atlas*, courtesy
Cristinerose Gallery

Jessica Craig-Martin
074 *Speed Boat Orgy, Venice
Bienale*, 1997
075 *Speed Boat Orgy, Venice
Bienale*, 1997
076 *Speed Boat Orgy, Venice
Bienale*, 1997

Katrina del Mar
115 *Bubblegum (Helen)*
116 *Sage with Half a Mustache
On (Hermaphrodite)*

Andrew Einhorn
092 *Luv Being Blonde*
093 *Meow*

Greg Friedler
020 *Untitled 1*
021 *Untitled 3*
022 *Untitled 2*

Sarah A. Friedman
094 *Pan_66*, from the series
Jack in Jack Off

Valerie Galloway
081 *Ethan Laughing*
082 *D&D*
083 *Afternoon*

Charles Gatewood
063 *Mountain Girl*, San
Francisco, 1994
064 *Joann and Anabel*, San
Francisco, 1995

Ralph Gibson
141 *Untitled*
142 *Untitled*

Nan Goldin
005 *Chloe in Hospital*, New
York, 1999
006 *Geno at Hotel*, Paris, 1999
007 *Clemens on Top of Jens,
Mouth Open*, Paris, 1999
008 *Nicola in the Shower*,
Paris, 1999

Janine Gordon
100 *Hold Back*, 1994
101 *Exile and Karen*, 1999
102 *Tied Up*, 1995
103 *Louis*, 1995

Peter J. Gorman
108 *Melissa on Bathroom
Floor*
109 *Portrait of Zrinka*
110 *Portrait of Pilar*

Frédéric Goudal (FiLH)
070 *Ashes*, 1998
071 *Plastic*, 1997
072 *One Knee*, 1997
073 *Pelvis*, 1996

Camella Grace
033 *2/*
034 *Toolgirl*
035 *Fire*
036 *Kathy Hires*

Lyle Ashton Harris
137 *Miss America*, 1987/88
138 *Untitled (Köln 1992)*, 1998
139 *Untitled (Michele 1984)*,
1998

Thomas Karsten
077 *Mira und Susen*
078 *Helen im Spiegel*
079 *Franziska*
080 *Franziska Mit Blumen*

Richard Kern
016 *Sean on Desk*, 1997
017 *Tracy in Hallway*, 1997
018 *Marissa's Toe*, 1998
019 *Lyle Sucks His Toe*, 1997

Marcelo Krasilcic
039 *Untitled*
040A *Untitled*
040B *Untitled*
041 *Untitled*
042 *Untitled*

David Levinthal
113 *Untitled*, from the series
Desire, 1990–91
114 *Untitled*, from the series
Desire, 1990–91

Richard Lohr
119 *C on Sofa*
120 *Caro*
121 *Blithe*

Leslie Lyons
025 *Egon Schiele Revisited I*
026 *Egon Schiele Revisited II*
027 *Susan I*
028 *Susan II*

Holger Maass
090 *Yellow*
091 *Green*

Vivienne Maricevic
117 *Joseph*
118 *Rex*

Robert Maxwell
045 *Penny/seated*
046 *Penny/rearview*
047 *Susan Touching on Couch*
048 *Susan's Sex*

Sean McDevitt
049 *Self-portrait at Kimba's*,
Athens, Georgia, 1993
050 *Self-portrait 136 Grand
Street*, Brooklyn, New
York, 1999
051 *Self-portrait 350 Megis
Street*, Athens, Georgia,
1994
052 *Self-portrait 163 Elkton
Road*, Newark, Delaware,
1996

Ian McFarlane
029 *Athens Bed*
030 *Jack's Mask*
031 *Katja Standing*
032 *Rest*

Sakiko Nomura
129 From the series *The Time
of Sensuous Light*, 1996
130 From the series *The Time
of Sensuous Light*, 1996
131 From the series *The Time
of Sensuous Light*, 1996
132 From the series *The Time
of Sensuous Light*, 1996

Valerie Phillips
098 *Untitled*
099 *Untitled*

George Pitts
122 *Rebecca*
123 *Untitled*
124 *Mfon*
125 *Mfon*

Sylvia Plachy
009 *Untitled*, Budapest, 1999
010 *Untitled*, Budapest, 1999
011 *Untitled*, Budapest, 1999
012 *Untitled*, Budapest, 1999

Terry Richardson
057 *Billy and Pearl*
058 *Tan Line '98*
059 *Soon Yi and Woody*
060 *Butts #2*

Chuck Samuels
111 *After Bullock*, Courtesy
Vance Martin
Photography/Edwyn Houk
Gallery
112 *After Newton*, Courtesy
Vance Martin
Photography/Edwin Houk
Gallery

Andres Serrano
143 *A History of Sex
(Alessandra)*, 1995,
courtesy Paula Cooper
Gallery
144 *A History of Sex
(Christiaan and Rose)*,
1996, courtesy Paula
Cooper Gallery
145 *A History of Sex (The
Kiss)*, 1996, courtesy
Paula Cooper Gallery

Taryn Simon
002 *Untitled*, courtesy Art and
Commerce
003 *Untitled*, courtesy Art and
Commerce
004 *Narcissus*, courtesy Art
and Commerce

Robert Stivers
023 *Color Series*, 1995/98
024 *Color Series*, 1987/98

Hiroshi Sunairi
067 *Hiroshima, Pour Bonne
Nuit*
068 *Basketball '79*
069 *Card Game*

Wolfgang Tillmans
126 *like praying I & II*, 1994,
courtesy Paula Cooper
Gallery
127 *Lutz & Alex, looking at
crotch*, 1991, courtesy
Paula Cooper Gallery
128 *Lutz & Alex, holding cock*,
1992, courtesy Paula
Cooper Gallery

Arthur Tress
061 *Lovers in a Kitchen*,
California, 1997
062 *Hermaphrodite*, East
Hampton, 1973

Barbara Vaughn
086 *Cracked Earth*
087 *Cracked Earth Series*
088 *Root System*
089 *Hondouras*

Tony Ward
013 *Tony and Pascale #386*
014 *Angel and Savannah #540*
015 *Blond Wig #137
Afro Wig #136*

Phillip Wong
065 *Roll, Roll, Roll*
066 *Eat Sheet*

Robert Zverina
084 *The Applicant*
085 *Angle of Repose*